John Carswell is Professorial Research Associate in the Department of the History of Art and Archaeology, SOAS, University of London. He was formerly Curator of the Oriental Institute at the University of Chicago and Director of the University's David and Alfred Smart Museum. He later served as Director of the Islamic and South Asian Department at Sotheby's. A graduate of the Royal College of Art, in his early career he worked on archaeological sites in Jericho, Greece and Turkey, before joining the Department of Fine Art at the American University of Beirut. He lives in London and Spain.

To Philippa

Speedy Motor

Travels across Asia and the
Middle East in a Morgan

John Carswell

I.B. TAURIS
LONDON · NEW YORK

Published in 2017 by
I.B.Tauris & Co. Ltd
London • New York
www.ibtauris.com

Copyright © 2017 John Carswell

The right of John Carswell to be identified as the author of this work has been asserted by the author in accordance with the Copyright, Designs and Patents Act 1988.

All rights reserved. Except for brief quotations in a review, this book, or any part thereof, may not be reproduced, stored in or introduced into a retrieval system, or transmitted, in any form or by any means, electronic, mechanical, photocopying, recording or otherwise, without the prior written permission of the publisher.

Every attempt has been made to gain permission for the use of the images in this book. Any omissions will be rectified in future editions.

References to websites were correct at the time of writing.

ISBN: 978 1 78453 726 5
eISBN: 978 1 78672 052 8
ePDF: 978 1 78673 052 7

A full CIP record for this book is available from the British Library
A full CIP record is available from the Library of Congress

Library of Congress Catalog Card Number: available

Typeset by Saxon Graphics Ltd, Derby
Printed and bound by CPI Group (UK) Ltd, Croydon, CR0 4YY

'Nothing matters now, except the **vow**
To steadfast my frame, shaky in its creams'

from 'The Distant Call', a poem by V. Vasu,
Kuwait Times, 1 July 1974

CONTENTS

List of Plates		viii
Map		x
What Visitors Should See		xii
1	In the Beginning	1
2	The Road to Damascus	13
3	Journey to Bombay	26
4	India to Sri Lanka	39
5	Sri Lanka	56
6	Male and the Maldives	69
7	Sri Lanka Again	95
8	India Once More	115
9	The Crash	137
10	Bombay and Back	151
11	War	163
12	After the War	178
Epilogue		189
Index of Names		191

PLATES

1. Chinese porcelain dish, from Damascus
2. M. Francois' driving instructions
3. Peggy and the Morgan in Beirut, across from the Intercontinental Hotel (left) and a nightclub (right)
4. John at Tabarja, across the bay from our house on the left
5. Inside our house at Tabarja, looking into our bedroom, the balcony and the bay on the left
6. The Waif: Andy with his broken arm in a sling
7. On the road: Speedy in the foreground, in the Taurus Mountains, Turkey
8. A close-up of Speedy, with Martha and Peggy, and Andy sitting on the bumper
9. Andy's interpretation of Speedy, driving at night
10. The Suq al-Hamidiyeh in Damascus. It was off an alley on the right that I found my first broken fourteenth-century Chinese blue-and-white dish
11. The fourteenth-century Chinese blue-and-white dish which nearly crashed onto the marble floor in Henri Pharaon's house in Beirut. It is now in the Art Institute of Chicago
12. In Kuwait, driving across the sand to SS *Dwarka*
13. Loading Speedy aboard, minus luggage and passengers

PLATES

14 In the jungle in south India, Andy discovered a group of extraordinary terracotta horses
15 In Male in the Maldives, the Hadibi mosque, looking down from our room in the Didi house. Note the scoops, of half coconut shells attached to long poles, on top of the well
16 Andy and a gang of Maldivian boys at the well
17 Mohamed Didi's gift of a model *dhoni*, complete with a moveable rudder, an anchor, oars and miniature fishing tackle
18 The real thing: a group of *dhonis* and fishermen in the harbour in Male
19 The celadon base sherd used as a stopper for a water jar
20 The white porcelain stem cup
21 A Maldivian lacquer box and cover containing cowry shells (*cipraea moneta*)
22 Maldivian carved coral gravestones in the cemetery adjacent to a mosque
23 A set of eight Persian Safavid seventeenth-century dishes and one later Chinese Swatow dish, purchased in Male by the author. Photo: Simon Chapman
24 A Maldivian Chess board purchased in Male by the author. Carved out a hard wood, probably teak, with designs resembling those on Maldivian gravestones; the red and yellow pieces are of typical local enamelled ware. Photo: Simon Chapman
25 The crash – the end of Speedy, with an amused spectator having his photo taken
26 We were befriended by a local family near Tarikere. Martha and Andy are on the left
27 Street scene in Beirut during the civil war
28 The envelope containing the invitation to the opening of the new Islamic Gallery at the Metropolitan Museum in New York. The Hezbollah had removed the stamps …

All images, unless stated otherwise, are the author's own.

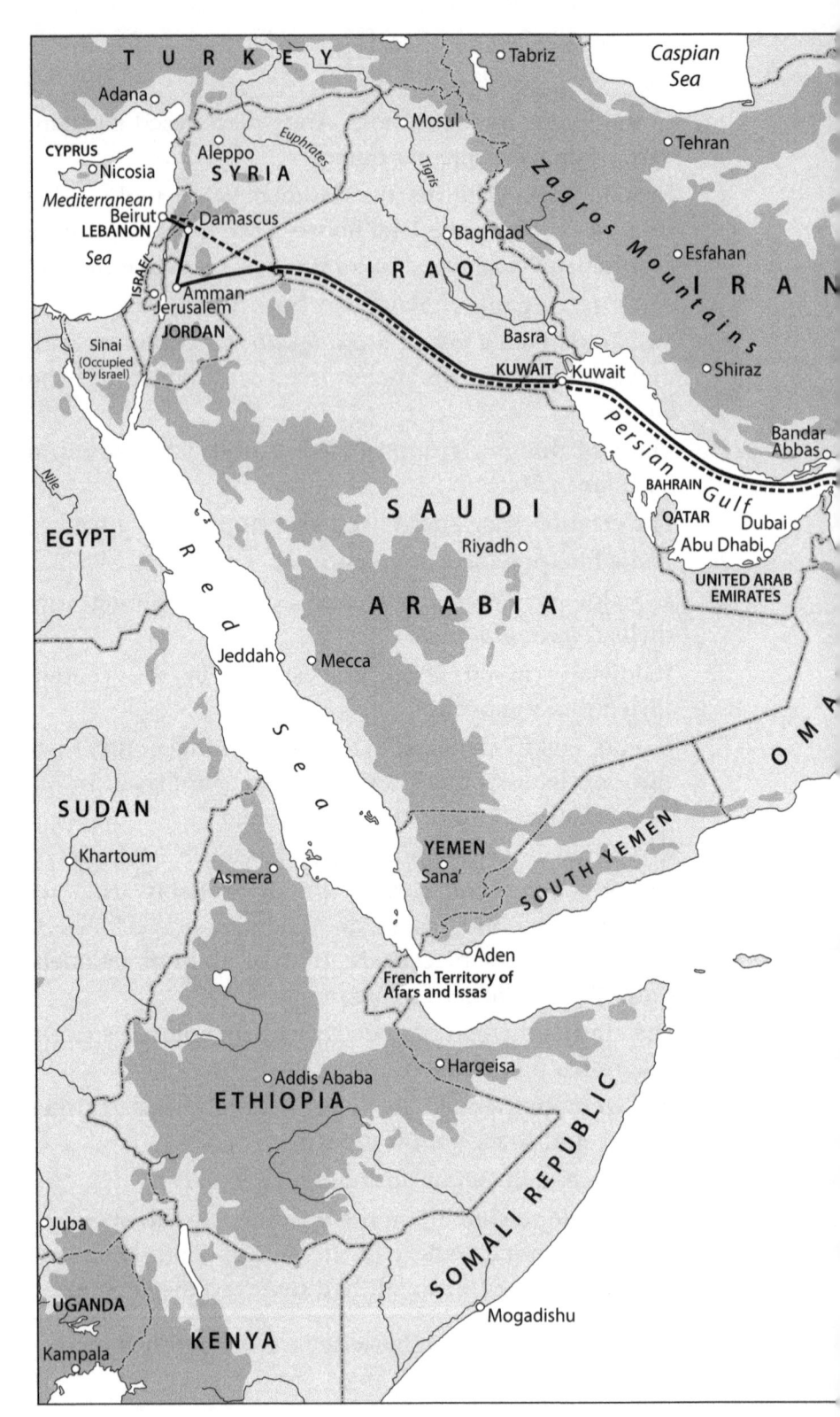

Speedy's journey, from Beirut to Male and back again, 1974

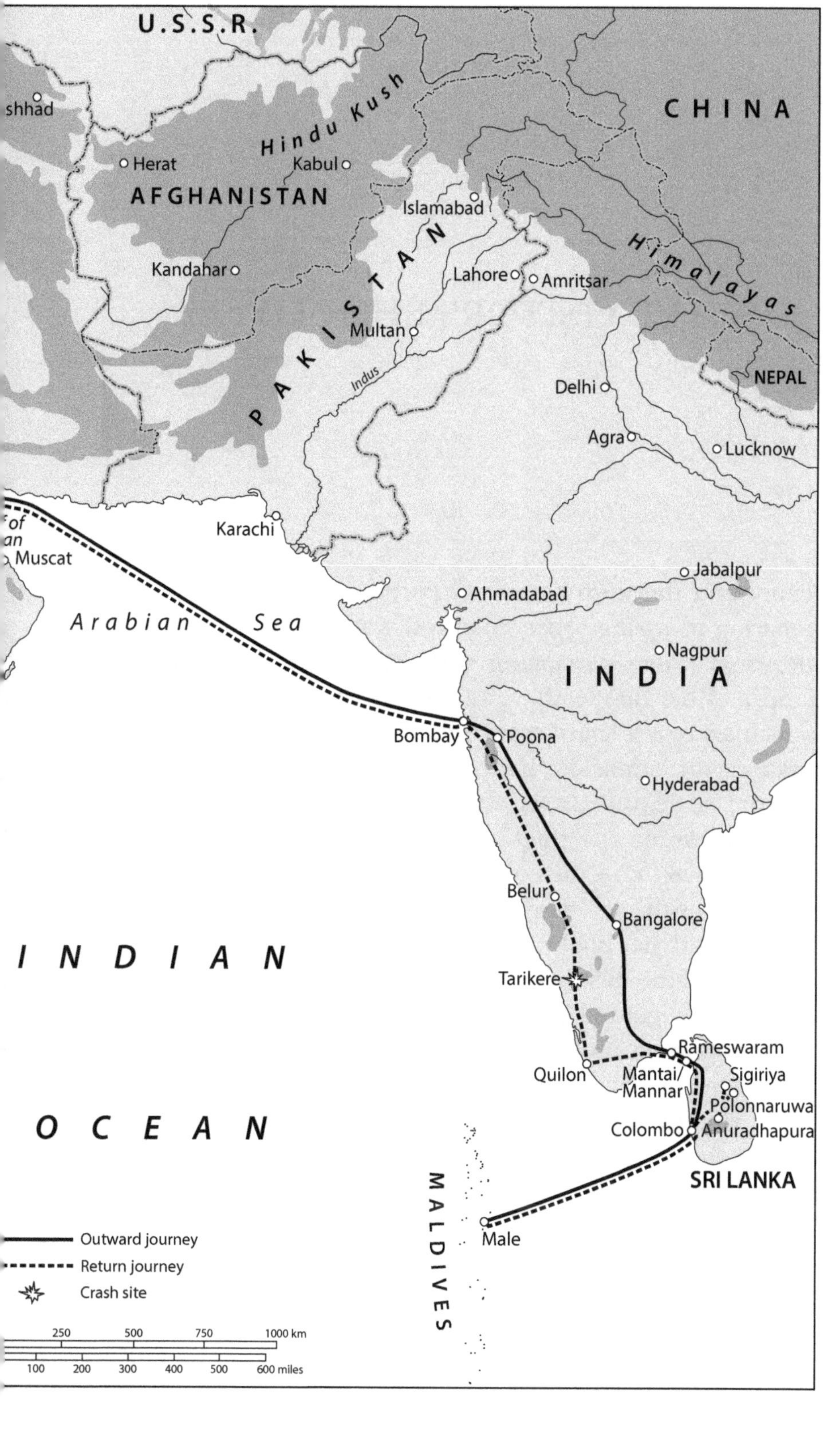
U.S.S.R.
shhad
Hindu Kush
CHINA
Herat
Kabul
AFGHANISTAN
Islamabad
PAKISTAN
Himalayas
Kandahar
Lahore
Amritsar
Multan
Indus
NEPAL
Delhi
Agra
Lucknow
Karachi
'of
an
Muscat
Jabalpur
Ahmadabad
Arabian Sea
Nagpur
INDIA
Bombay
Poona
Hyderabad
Belur
Bangalore
INDIAN
Tarikere
Rameswaram
Quilon
Mantai/
Mannar
Sigiriya
Polonnaruwa
Colombo
Anuradhapura
OCEAN
SRI LANKA
MALDIVES
Male
Outward journey
Return journey
Crash site
250
500
750
1000 km
100
200
300
400
500
600 miles

WHAT VISITORS SHOULD SEE

Beauty and the mirror, the pet parrot ... Vasantha – a lady preparing to syringe rose coloured water upon her lover ... The song: a damsel singing with her mouth open giving a glimpse of her fine teeth ... a fly sits on a small jack fruit and an inch away is a lizard crunching to spring on its prey ... the **vina-damsel** admiring her cursl ... the huntress with a petticoat of leaves ... the seven horses on his chariot are driven by Aruna the thighless brother of Garuda ... Arjuna looking dawn into a dish of oil and shooting an arrow into the eyes of a fish ... many interesting and graceful figures, Huntress with her big brum dance ... lady giving an exhibition of the art of the gesture ... the drum dence ... the toe ring a royal lady is getting a ring put on her toe dvan attendant attempting to balance herself on one leg.

The song a musician singing with symbols in her hand, mouth slightly open with lovely smile, lyasa dance, damcel keeping time with her left foot slightip raised, a bee sucking honey from the flowering creeper over her head.

Belur and Halebid, Tourist Printers,
Evening Bazaar, Mysore

1

IN THE BEGINNING

SOME PEOPLE ought not to have anything to do with motor cars, and events over the past few years would suggest that I am one of those people. Actually, the first wheeled vehicle which I had anything to do with was my pram, and I remember being more intrigued by the simulated basket-work decoration on the interior – very much along the lines of that which occurs in a number of Picasso's collages – than its gently rocking progress. About the same time, I ran across the road in front of the suburban house where we lived in order to buy an ice cream, in front of an oncoming car. There was a scream of brakes and the car skidded forward, just enough to bonk me over in the road, unhurt. I can only have been about three or so, but it was a good lesson learned early on that cars could be lethal.

This aesthetic interest in four-wheeled vehicles was to be my undoing some years later on, and in a funny way was to prove to be the genesis of this book. I was teaching art at the American University of Beirut in Lebanon, in those halcyon days between two civil wars. It must have been about 1965, and I fell in love with the lines of a gleaming white Alfa Romeo, a Spider, which I saw in a car sale room in the city. With the help of a friendly bank manager I bought it. But there was a slight problem: I didn't know how to drive.

But it really wasn't a problem, for a colleague where I was teaching at the university was a car buff, and deeply impressed with my purchase, gallantly offered to teach me. We went for one or two precarious excursions, after which he confided in his wife that as far as he was concerned, I was a non-starter, and perhaps she should take over. I can't remember the exact sequence of events, but they must have been sufficiently alarming for her, a good wife and mother of three, for her to also throw in the sponge. I do remember giving a lift to an archaeologist lady-friend at one stage, who politely pointed out that after a quarter of a mile or so, one half of the car was still on the pavement.

I then fell into the professional clutches of a Lebanese instructor, M. François. Nothing if not thorough, he had had a manual printed for his pupils, a copy of which I still possess. I quote:

Q. If four meet on four cross roads, who should pass first?
A. The four should stop and agree which one should pass before, and then the one whose right becomes follows.

Q. Why should you put your hand on the klaxon?
A. So that no passenger jumps suddenly out of the tram in front of the car.

Q. How can you know that the road is wide between the tram line and the foot path, so that to pass or stop?
A. I take my right towards the foot path and see if there are seventy centimeters between the edge of my car and the tram line, this proves that the road is wide.

Q. If you smell a bad smell, what does it mean?
A. There might be a contact or the silk is burning or the brake is tied or the clutch is loose.

I am glad to report that M. François' strictures never had the slightest effect on his Lebanese students, who to this day drive with a self-interested verve that can only lead to civil strife. After the last round of the civil war, the story circulating in Beirut was about a Lebanese lady who went to Europe for the first time after seventeen years of bloody conflict, and returned astonished to report that in Europe they were so backward that they had to have coloured lights to tell them when to stop and start.

Anyhow, for my instruction, I was decanted from the Alfa and into M. François' jeep, and driven eternally round a car park behind the local supermarket. After a certain time and with a number of lessons elapsed and paid for, the moment came for the test. This took place on a notoriously steep hill just south of Beirut, on a kilometre of specially dedicated road. Still in the jeep, we joined a flock of other jeeps, all manned by Lebanese ladies. I don't think Lebanese men ever deigned to be examined – there were other, simpler ways of getting a licence. Because taking the test was a trauma (it certainly was for me), it bore a distinct resemblance to going to hospital in Lebanon, that is, the whole extended family turned up as well, to rejoice or console. Brakeless ladies would reverse into unexpected parking places and end up in chaos at the bottom of that dreaded hill. Others more triumphant would make it into the allotted space. The wails of the fallen intermingled with the shrieks of the successful – in both cases, the ladies were carried off – in victory or to doom.

Thoroughly sobered by what I saw, I was extra cautious and progressed at less than snail's pace, reversing and performing the rest of the ritual. I passed. Except that there was now a real problem, for (a) I had never once driven in traffic, which in Beirut can only be compared to a bull fight and (b) I had never driven anything except M. François' jeep, and certainly not my beautiful, brand-new, sparkling white Spider. But with all the insouciance of youth, I leapt into my motor and away I went, again I must admit for a considerable distance on the sidewalk; no matter, Beirutis are used to this. My American friend Ritchie, who had observed this performance, was however thoroughly alarmed and told his wife Peggy over dinner that night that I would most surely soon come to a sticky end.

Instead, the summer came, and as the university moved into a languorous vacation, I decided this was the moment to drive back home to London in my beautiful Spider. I did have the good sense to realise that Syria, Turkey and Anatolia, Bulgaria and the land of the Slavs might prove a little taxing for my incipient skills, so I put the car and myself on a smart Italian liner for Genoa. I actually managed to get as far as the port of Beirut under my own control, and the voyage was pleasantly uneventful. I slept soundly in the knowledge that my sleek new motor was safely stowed away below the decks and could come to no harm. As the boat approached the shore, I began to get a bit apprehensive about what lay ahead, but I needn't have worried. For whom, when I stepped down the gangplank, should I see waving bravely but the wife of my American friend. Convinced by Ritchie that I would indeed kill myself if I set out alone in the Spider, she had abandoned her husband and family to make sure that I didn't. I married her.

I did, eventually, learn to drive the Alfa, and became exceedingly enamoured of its ability to take off at high speed, and its capacities in fifth gear; I lost quite a few headlamps in the initial stages. For the next couple of years, it became a ritual to drive back and forth from Beirut to London during the summer time. Besides learning to drive, I was also learning to adjust to an instant family – my new wife Peggy, and the three children she brought along with her, Kathy (12), Martha (9) and Andrew (5). Like most inexperienced stepfathers, I had some imaginative ideas about how to translate from confirmed bachelorhood to benevolent paternalism. I remember one incident particularly that was less than successful. I decided that I would entertain the children by driving them up to the snows above the Cedars of Lebanon, and then take them higher still in the chair lift and set off fireworks in the snowy peaks to amuse them. Unfortunately they were already grown up enough not to fit neatly into the space behind the two front seats, and bright blue with cold they shrieked and howled in horror and exasperation. This was not repeated.

We were living at that time – as indeed we did until we had to leave Lebanon a decade later – in a wonderful old Lebanese house, built right on the beach of a little fishing village called Tabarja, some twenty miles north of Beirut. It had a central room with three great arches and a balcony above the sea, twenty feet below. The ceilings were twenty feet high, and the whole inside painted white. The sense of space and light was impressive even for an adult, but one had no idea how alarming it must have been for the children, after the security of a modern Beirut apartment. The two girls had one of the corner front rooms, facing the sea, and Peggy and I the opposite one. Andy was cast into a back room, but again with a doorway facing the balcony. A long corridor ran right across the house, off which (besides Andy's room) opened a dining-room, my study, the kitchen and little bathroom. Upstairs, there was access by a wooden staircase from the kitchen to an attic, and the flat roof.

I had lived in the house for a number of years, having first found it on an excursion to the village in 1957. It was absolutely traditional in style, a style which has been said to derive from Venetian *palazzi*, but which you can find down the whole coast of the Levant, from Aleppo to Gaza. Built of stone, the houses are surprisingly cool in summer and warm in winter, and the view from the balcony of ours was spectacular, looking down on the little fisherman's bay, with a tiny church to the left and a cottage on the rocks to the right. There always seemed to be a boat, drawn on an imaginary string, slowly crossing the western horizon. Behind, the village of similar but more modest houses rose steeply through orange groves to the mountains above. Narcissus, anemones and cyclamen grew wild and in profusion.

When I first arrived in the village there was no electricity, and I lived by the light of a pressure lamp. I also learned to go to bed when it got dark, and get up when the sun rose; this was a habit difficult to break later in life when I moved back to the civilised world. It was also a very noisy village, for it was dedicated to fishing at night, so every evening there was a great clatter on the beach with much shouting and swearing as the boats were launched from the shingle below.

The house had a curious history, for it was built before World War I by my landlord's father, who had made a pile in South America and then returned home. He only lived in it for a year or so, as he went mad, and his wife refused to live in it after he died. It was then shut up until World War II, when General Weygand had it as his headquarters of the French military mission. For reasons not clear, its typical tiled, pitched roof got blown off by a bomb, and it lay roofless for another ten years until just before I arrived, when my present landlord had it re-roofed in concrete. The stone ornament was in the strict classical tradition of the Near East, stretching back to Palmyra and Baalbeck, with elegantly carved pediments and mouldings, *oeil de boeuf* windows and arches above the doors with dog-tooth ornament. With its flat roof, the total effect was surprisingly Georgian. As I am a painter, it couldn't have been a better artist's house. Apart from pictures and sculpture, there wasn't much in the way of furniture, except a twenties' gramophone which boomed out Vivaldi and the like; a friend once remarked I had the campest selection of records in the Levant. There was also a stuffed elephant, which I had acquired second-hand from the museum of the American University.

The absence of furniture and the presence of the elephant was also somewhat daunting for the children. Their integration into the house was a problem, for I was determined not to spoil the aesthetic effect. Serviceable cupboards and beds were inserted where they could not be seen from the main room; it must have been strange for the children to find they had to perform quite ordinary functions hidden behind half-closed doors. They did, however, rather take to the elephant, as indeed their children have now done many years later.

IN THE BEGINNING

The two girls were at school in Beirut, so they got tucked into the Alfa every day with me, to drive to the University. Andy was sent to a village school (entirely Arabic) at a tender age, and then later carted off by bus to a French school in Jounieh, a few miles in the direction of Beirut. As he spoke neither language, he was remarkably sanguine about this experience, though it didn't do much for his education. Their father Ritchie was still living in Beirut, and himself got married again shortly afterwards, so the relationships remained guardedly amicable. Peggy's parents lived in the States, on the west coast, and mine in London, so the summers got fairly complicated with multiple obligations and not much money to fulfil them. We became expert in travelling by strange East European airlines – the children thought nothing of changing planes in Moscow or Bucharest en route for Seattle – and Peggy was the acknowledged authority in Beirut on what was euphemistically known as the 'tricky ticket'.

And there was, of course, always the Alfa. It was Andy who decided it should be called 'Speedy Motor', a name which has stuck. And it was he and his sister Martha who solved the delicate problem of what to call me; I couldn't be Dad, because I wasn't, and they couldn't call me John, because that was what their mother used. So I became Tommy, which was acceptable to all, and has remained so ever since. The first summer we drove to London alone, the children posted on later. In London, we had a flat in Westminster, and that summer was enlivened by a couple of crashes, neither of them I hasten to say through any fault of mine. Cruising along The Mall one day in the direction of Admiralty Arch, we were overtaken by a coach load of musical guardsmen, on their way to play for the Queen Mother at her birthday lunch. The driver turned sharp left to Marlborough House across my bow, which was neatly demolished. The Alfa was out of commission for a while whilst it was rebuilt in Putney. I had barely got it back and the insurance claim settled, when I was driving down Holborn, and spotting a red light ahead, stopped. The only trouble was that the lorry immediately behind me didn't, and wiped out the rear end of the car. The boys in the Alfa garage could barely restrain their mirth when I returned to have it rebuilt again, which I thought was fairly uncharitable of them.

Back in Beirut nothing particularly dramatic happened, except perhaps an Easter trip to Palmyra across the Syrian desert, when the engine conked out and we had to be towed to Tartus in the dark by a friendly peasant with a tractor. The summer came round again, and as the children were now definitely too large to stow away, we sent them on ahead to their grandparents, and set off once more overland to Europe in the Alfa. This all went wonderfully smoothly, and we traversed Syria and Turkey without a problem, having some memorable picnics on the way. We purred through Bulgaria, and Yugoslavia presented no trouble, though Peggy was nearly demolished by a very large rock which fell from a mountain pass just inches below her head. We arrived in Trieste feeling rather pleased with ourselves, and a terrific lunch in Venice was the prelude for a most exhilarating sweep down the autostrade at well over 100 mph, the fastest I had ever been. I managed to calm down by dusk, by which time we had reached the ancient town of Bergamo. I drove up to the front door of a smartish hotel and booked a room for the night. Was there a garage?, I enquired. Oh no, they said, just park outside in the street. We were exhausted, and after locking everything up in the car took a minimum of luggage upstairs to our room. After a dinner of porcini of massive proportions, we collapsed into bed, tired and content.

The next morning there was a problem. There was no car. It had been spirited away during the night. Worst of all, so had all our clothes, Peggy's jewellery, presents for the children, and most mortifying for me, the entire manuscript and illustrations of a book I had just written about Chinese porcelain found in Syria, including two unique pieces I had just purchased in Damascus. We implored the police to help and put advertisements in the Bergamo press asking for the contents and we would forget the car. All to no avail, and to this day I have a vision of Mr and Mrs Thief sitting happily at supper, with a new Alfa (Italians *like* Alfas), jewels for her and presents for *their* children. The Chinese porcelain never surfaced on the open market, and I suspect with the manuscript got dumped in the nearest canal. Anyhow, after several fruitless days, we finally realised there was nothing to be done, and slunk off to the railway station to buy two one-way tickets to London.

I never really recovered from the loss of the Alfa, and to this day my heart beats faster when I see a Spider in the street, particularly if it is a white one. But by this time I had become definitely mobile, and we obviously had to have something to replace it. Means were short so we had to scale down our sights somewhat, and eventually settled for a Triumph Spitfire, in a rather unappealing shade of dark blue. This was even less accommodating for extra passengers, and returning to Beirut a lot of our travel from then on was done by taking seats in *service* taxis. There was a good *service* back and forth from Tabarja to Beirut, and Kathy and Martha got adept at taking it. Again at Easter, we made a trip in the Spitfire with Tony Daniels, a painter friend, across the Syrian desert to Baghdad. This was an extraordinary adventure, for it snowed in the desert and we had a struggle to make it along the deeply rutted tracks. Tony, being quite tall, spent most of the journey leaning out the back waving at passing camel-trains and trying to keep warm. There were some other surreal moments, circling the spiral minaret at Samarra, the early Abbasid capital on the Tigris, and driving through the *suqs* of Baghdad. But the Spitfire never really made it in my imagination, and the following summer we put an advertisement in a London paper and sold it to a young man in Leeds, for cash. We returned to London by train.

Now what? Well, another vision had crossed my threshold. This was a Morgan; and when I was told I could have a white one if I wanted it, I made a down payment immediately. Also, as a family man, I was told there was a 4/4 four seater, which seemed ideal.

Buying a Morgan is an experience which has been many times recounted by others, and our own foray turned out to be wonderfully typical. We took the train to Malvern Link, a little Victorian station, now so reduced that it was entirely managed by one man. We asked him the way to the factory. 'Well', he said, 'just cut across the common there and when you get to the blackberry bushes, take a sharp left turn and it's at the bottom of the hill'. We did.

We were confronted with a long, low brick building with a single door. We entered, and found a sort of waiting room, furnished with a bench and photographs of early exploits, rallies and races. There was a serving hatch to the right, and a bell beside it, which we rang. After a longish interval, the hatch shot up and a woman peered out and rather grimly asked us what our business might be? 'We want to buy a Morgan', we said. 'Ah', she replied, 'you need the sales manager; I'll send him round immediately', and slammed the hatch down with a bang. A few minutes later, the front door opened, and in came the rep., a charming man with a harelip. Would we like a tour of the factory first? We would indeed, and set off on the classic trip, starting with the timber-yard (Morgans have a wooden frame) and inspecting the Belgian ash – tricky to use as it often contained bits of shrapnel from World War I, which as he said, played hell with the planes.

Morgans appear to be entirely assembled from boxes of spare parts and the atmosphere resembles nothing so much as a children's playroom full of happy adults. Once mounted, the chassis is then pushed around from one shed to another by hand. The canvas hood is marked, cut and stitched by a kind elderly tailor, with two lady assistants working an ancient sewing machine. Indeed, much of the equipment is original and has never been superseded by anything better; for instance, the guillotine for cutting the parallel louvres on the bonnet, themselves marked out with a pencil and ruler. Whilst the engines are standard, and ordered from elsewhere, the suspension is most certainly not, and is quite unique. Riding a Morgan has been compared to driving across a rutted field in winter; you do indeed most certainly get a feeling for the road.

I have never seen a happier workforce; for me this was epitomised by a band of young men, their shirts off in the sunshine, sanding down the cars for the nth time, prior to them being enamelled, with obvious enjoyment. And what colours! In the final shed, ranks of cars in orange, yellow, scarlet, green, anything you could think of. There had, of course, been many attempts and suggestions as to how the factory could be rationalised and streamlined into the twentieth century. These were met by the management, and I guess by the workforce too, with amused titters. The Morgan family was then in its third generation, and thank god not likely to change. Refinements, yes, but the basic style was set; the lengthy waiting list was proof enough that nobody wants it to change, anyway.

When the great day came a couple of years later to collect ours, it was indeed a cause for celebration. We zoomed out of Malvern Link in the direction of London, and never looked back, although many motorists passing in the opposite direction did so – never was there a car which attracts so much benevolent attention and good humour on the open road. This continued throughout Europe and Asia, till we once again returned to Beirut, in the summer of 1971. Perhaps the most spectacular section of road on the whole trip is that between Konya and Antalya in Turkey, between mountains and rushing rivers, and I was moved enough to stop and take a photograph of Andy, grinning from ear to ear and sitting on the running board during that royal progress back home, with Martha and his mother in the background. Back in Beirut, the Morgan turned many heads too, and it was considered an ornament, whether sitting across the road in Tabarja under a mulberry tree, or on the campus of the American University parked under a banyan. In fact the only disenchanted note came surprisingly from my mother, who found entry and exit from the passenger seat a trial; never known to have uttered a swear word in her entire life, she was overheard to refer to it on one occasion as 'that bloody car', and cornered Peggy in the kitchen and tried to talk her into persuading me to exchange it for something more 'sensible'.

2

THE ROAD TO DAMASCUS

IT WAS IN BEIRUT in the early seventies that I made a discovery which was to substantially alter the rest of my life. As an art historian, I had become particularly interested in the evolution of Turkish pottery, and Islamic ceramics in general. Working on fifteenth-century tiles from Syria, Egypt and Turkey, hexagonal in shape and decorated in blue and white, I couldn't help noticing that not only in their colour scheme, but also in their designs, they were obviously influenced by contemporary Chinese porcelain. At just about this moment, I zoomed round the corner in downtown Beirut on my way to work, and spotted a Chinese blue-and-white bowl in the window of Khalil Sarkis's antique shop, just opposite the famous St Georges Hotel. I slammed on the brakes (luckily, for once, there was nothing immediately behind me) and stopped to inspect it, and ended up buying it for no great sum. It was a typical sixteenth-century bowl, and I was curious enough to ask Khalil where it had come from. He told me it was from his brother Elie, who had another shop, in Damascus. After a couple of weeks or so I set off with Peggy for Damascus – a pleasant day's drive across the mountains of Lebanon and the Anti-Lebanon, and the Bekaa Valley. In Damascus, we found other examples for sale in the *suq*, concentrated, of all places, in the Singer Sewing Machine shop, where peasant women were bringing them in part exchange for new machines. Elie Sarkis confirmed that it was all coming from Douma, a village some ten kilometres away on the edge of the *ghuta*, or gardens of Damascus.

Douma is traditionally the village from which come the entrepreneurs who manage the vast gardens for the Damascene landlords, and have since time immemorial taken a 40 per cent profit. This means that the Doumiani are surprisingly rich themselves, although their personality is to remain self-effacing to the point of obscurity. They live in mud-brick houses and dress in mud-coloured clothes, and fade into the general landscape. It is well known in political circles in Syria that if your star should fall, you retire to Douma until things get better again. As for material possessions, when you enter a house in Douma, singularly unprepossessing on the outside, it is to find a wealth of decoration – painted woodwork, *objets d'art*, and almost always a cabinet full of knick-knacks, artificial flowers, a transistor radio … and Chinese porcelain.

However, all this changed in the late sixties thanks to the late President Hafez El-Assad. He decided to modernise Douma, built a new two-lane highway from Damascus and a new post office, and more importantly a clutch of new apartment blocks. When the inhabitants of Douma left their old – and spacious – mud-brick villas they found that they had rather more possessions than would fit into a modern apartment, so there was a general *nettoyage*. Initially, the Chinese porcelain would be lodged with a local shopkeeper, who would then negotiate with Elie Sarkis and the like for its sale. The owners, of course, had no idea of its antiquity; as Chinese porcelain shows little signs of age, at best they would remember it had been handed down from their grandparents' time, little knowing that some of it dated back to the fourteenth century. In fact, the whole range of Chinese blue-and-white from its incipience in the first quarter of the fourteenth century till our own times was represented by the eight hundred or more pieces of porcelain that came to light in Syria in the early seventies. What started as a trickle became a flood, and the dealers in Damascus moved it on to Beirut, and ultimately the rest of the world. It was somewhat surprising at that time to walk down the Suq Al-Hamadieh and be accosted by Syrian merchants who would hiss 'Mink! Mink!' conspiratorially in your ear. I bought a number of pieces myself, mostly broken, and had a lucky find when I discovered a large fourteenth-century dish in a second-hand clothes shop, underneath a pair of trousers.

Although Chinese porcelain was certainly not my academic interest at that time, I realised that this sudden wave of new material was important, and that if I did not document it, no one else would. I came to an arrangement with Elie and his brother Khalil in Beirut that in return for telling them what it was and its approximate value, they would let me draw and photograph every piece. They also helped me by telling me to whom they had previously sold pieces, and who had started to form collections of it. In fact, in this fashion I located more than twenty separate owners. I was also quite fortuitously responsible for the formation of the two major collections of Chinese porcelain from Syria, each with over two hundred examples.

The first belonged to Henri Pharaon, already a distiguished collector in his own right of Islamic material. Henri Pharaon owned one of the leading banks in Beirut and controlled the port, and was exceedingly rich. He was also an important *éminence grise* in the labyrinthine intrigues of Lebanese political life, respected by all parties and always trying to stitch together an acceptable coalition of the warring factions. He was actually the scion of a noble family from Trieste, the Faroni, who had become tax gatherers in Egypt before moving to Lebanon in the nineteenth century. His father, equally prosperous, built a mansion in Beirut in Italianate Gothic style and filled it full of furniture from Mappin and Webb in London.

As a young man, Henri Pharaon developed a life-long passion for Arab horses and racing, and he used to visit Syria frequently in his quest for bloodstock for his stables. It was in Syria that he became aware of the lavishly decorated interiors of the older Syrian houses, and when he inherited his father's Edwardian pile he stripped out the whole of the interior, and over the years built into it the carved and painted wooden interiors of more than twenty Syrian houses, ranging from the sixteenth century onwards, along with marble floors and fountains.

Henri Pharaon was short in stature, lame and had a terrible birthmark covering most of his face; ugly as sin, he was also one of the most generous and astute men I have ever met. When I first arrived in Beirut in 1956, he learned that I was interested in Islamic art and invited me from time to time to look at his potential purchases. He was, of course, well known to all the dealers and got first refusal on anything that turned up in Beirut, whether legally or not. His garden, which was as palatial as his house, was stacked with classical columns and wind-blown acanthus leaf capitals ripped off from famous Syrian sites such as Apamea and Qalat Simaan.

One day he telephoned me at the University and asked me to stop by on his way home; he had a whole collection of Islamic ceramics on offer. He showed me it spread out on the double bed in one of his guest rooms. But what caught my eye was a magnificent Chinese fourteenth-century blue-and-white plate, perched precariously on the edge of the silk counterpane and just about to fall on the marble floor. He was unaware that it was anything special, indeed even that it was Chinese, until I told him about its age and value. This led to him to start making a large collection of porcelain, with the help of the Syrian dealers, and being a true collector by nature he became something of a connoisseur. Again, I was allowed to draw and photograph the porcelain as it accrued.

I became such a frequent visitor to the Pharaon house that one day he said to stop ringing him up before coming, and just let myself in; the servants, after all, knew who I was. I took him up on this and often used to call early in the morning, as his house was on my way in to work at the University.

Once I remember whilst cataloguing away I heard an extraordinary clicking noise in the next room. I went to investigate, to find Henri Pharaon hard at work with his trainer crouched above a backgammon board. Like everything he did, he took his *tric-trac* seriously, and every day before breakfast he would have a session with a professional player.

A decade or so later, when the civil war broke out in earnest in Lebanon, his house was close to the major area of fighting. But he refused to leave, saying that if everyone stayed at home things would quickly resolve themselves. He showed great personal bravery as he had no one in the house except his two servants, one of whom had his throat slit. He told me that another time, two Muslims ran into his garden to take refuge; he invited them in, and phoned Chamoun, the head of the Christian faction, who promised to send a tank to make sure they got back safely to their own quarter. Instead, a band of Christian militiamen broke his front door down and shot them dead in front of him; as he said, what was particularly dishonourable was the fact that they were drinking *his* coffee at the time. But, in spite of all the horror, his collecting instinct never failed, and when I visited him on another occasion during the war he invited me in to see his *new* collection. This consisted of bombs and shrapnel that had hit the house or fallen in the garden. 'Look at this', he said, 'it's American, and that one's Israeli, and this Russian ...'. He had them all classified and neatly displayed in the hall.

The second largest collection of Chinese porcelain from Syria began in a similarly fortuitous way. I was riding back from Damascus one day in a *service* taxi carrying a Chinese bowl, and who should be in the next seat but an old friend from Beirut, Theo Larsson. Theo was the son of Swedish fundamentalist Christians who had emigrated first to the United States and then to the Holy Land. They had expected the end of the world to come in 1900, and thought the best place to be would be Jerusalem for that cataclysmic event. As nothing happened, they decided to settle in Jerusalem, and his father became the Swedish Consul. Theo grew up in Jerusalem and learned fluent Arabic as a child, and pursued various business interests in Palestine and Transjordan throughout the war. Two of his major claims to fame were that it was his car in which Count Bernadotte was assassinated by the Stern Gang in 1948 – Theo was his aide-de-camp – and it was also his stolen revolver which was used by an Arab terrorist to murder King Abdullah.

Theo asked me what I was carrying, and I explained to him what it was, and where it had come from. His appetite was whetted and with his excellent Arabic was able to track down another two hundred or so pieces in Damascus, and also became very knowledgeable about the subject. My reward, again, was to be allowed to draw and photograph them, and one day I received a call from Theo in Beirut asking me to breakfast. He and his wife lived at that time in a charming little two-storey old Lebanese house in a large garden in Ras Beirut, once with a view of the sea but soon to be swamped by high-rise apartments. When I arrived, he let me discover for myself what he had propped up on the mantelpiece. It was another magnificent fourteenth-century dish, with a unique design at the centre of a pair of ducks and a little flotilla of ducklings in a lotus-pond. He told me that it had changed hands at least half a dozen times in the past twenty-four hours, from its discovery in an old house in the Salahiyeh quarter of Damascus, until he acquired it. Many years later, Guiseppe Eskenazi sold it in London.

Many of the finest pieces eventually turned up on the international market, and it was amusing when I finally went to work for Sotheby's to see pieces which I had seen before in altogether different circumstances. One such was an early fifteenth-century bowl, of a very rare type which had been intended to be decorated in red, but which had misfired to a very beautiful grey. This I had seen, of all places, in the caretaker's room of the Sursock Museum in Beirut, where it was used under the sink in which to keep dirty dishcloths. I pointed out to the Director of the Museum, Ibrahim Beyhum, that although it might be a sign of true aristocracy (and the Sursocks were certainly that) to have such a bowl delegated to washing up, it really deserved a better fate. I forget I had said this until some years later it, too, turned up for sale in London.

Another piece eventually found a proper niche in London. This was a remarkable blue-and-white cylindrical stand with a flaring rim and base, also early fifteenth century. This I found amongst a private collection in Damascus, belonging to a Syrian physician, Dr Aractingi, who had collected Chinese ware over the years just because he liked it. What was so unusual about the stand was its form and decoration, which were clearly derived from a Mamluk inlaid metal prototype, which must have travelled to the Far East to be copied in turn in Chinese blue-and-white porcelain, to be exported to Syria, perhaps as a diplomatic present. What was so strange was the fact that the Chinese potter had not only attempted to replicate the Islamic ornament, but also the original Arabic inscription which encircled the stand. I published the stand in *Oriental Art*, along with the kinds of Mamluk brass stands which must have been its prototype.

A year or so later I was in the British Museum and went to see my friend and mentor Basil Gray, then Keeper of Oriental Antiquities. Basil was a pioneer, for his interests ranged across the whole of Asia, and he was equally at home with Far Eastern, Indian and Islamic material. We chatted for half an hour or so, and just as I was about to leave, he told me that they had acquired something which might interest me. He opened a polished mahoghany cupboard in his office, and there on the top shelf was the stand. Apparently Dr Aractingi had died, and his nephew had flown to London with the piece in a suitcase and offered it to the museum, which Basil told me they had bought for no great sum of money.

By 1972, my catalogue of Chinese porcelain from Syria reached over six hundred items, and I was seriously hooked on the subject. On my visits back to England I tried to find out as much as I could about the subject, studying the major museum collections. I realised that the Syrian material lay exactly between two other great collections of Chinese porcelain – that which had belonged to the Ottoman Sultans and which was now housed in the Topkapi Sarayi in Istanbul, and that which had been used at the Safavid court, then donated to the Shrine of Sheikh Safi at Ardebil on the Caspian Sea by Shah Abbas I, and finally moved into storage in the National Museum in Tehran. The Topkapi porcelain was well known, though not in its entirety till published some years later by Regina Krahl in three great folio volumes. The Ardebil collection less so, though the Director of the Freer Gallery in Washington DC, John Pope, wrote a monograph on it. He was also responsible for identifying the characteristics of the earliest fourteenth-century Chinese wares, based on the strong representation of this period in the Topkapi collection. The Turkish and Persian collections were royal collections, and what made the Syrian material so interesting was the fact that this must have been the kind of porcelain in everyday use amongst the Syrian bourgeoisie. It must have always been considered valuable for a large number of Syrian pieces were broken, but had been riveted back together again.

Why was Chinese porcelain so sought after in the Near East and the Islamic world in general? The answer can only be its unique quality; porcelain and the secret of its manufacture was a Chinese monopoly for over a thousand years. There is a fundamental difference between porcelain and ordinary glazed pottery. Porcelain is made of petuntse and kaolin, that is pulverised china-stone and white china-clay, both of which were mined near the great manufacturing centre at Jingdezen, in south central China. The two elements, both of which ultimately come from decomposed granite, form the body of the ware, which is fired at a high temperature, c. 1,280°F. to form a hard, pure white stoneware. One of its characteristics is that when thin, it is translucent, and another that when struck it rings like a bell. The glaze is of similar composition as the body, and when fired fuses with the body so it is impossible to tell where one begins and the other ends. Further, when you break a piece of blue-and-white porcelain, it also tends to have conchoidal fractures, that is it splinters just like a shell.

Pottery, on the other hand is simply made from ordinary clay, and fired at a much lower temperature. If glazed, the lead or tin glaze tends to lie on the surface of the body as a separate skin, although various kinds of flux allow it to adhere to a better extent. And if you wish to cover up the colour of the earthenware body, then it is necessary to dress the body with an opacifying white slip. There has been a long tradition of glazed pottery in the Near East since at least classical times, and from the early Islamic period it became increasingly more sophisticated both in composition and decoration with different coloured glazes, particularly in Persia and Syria in the early medieval period. But the arrival in the Near East of opaque white Chinese stonewares in the early Abbasid period, corresponding to the Tang dynasty (618–907) in China, baffled the Islamic potters, though they soon began to try to imitate them in more humble pottery. So did the porcelain of the Song dynasty (960–1279), which was again imitated in Saljuk white wares. But the real crunch came in the early fourteenth century, with the massive import of Chinese blue-and-white porcelain.

Here, the blue decoration is of paramount importance, for the cobalt blue was itself initially of Persian origin. The Persian potters had used blue for centuries before, and it has been speculated that it was Persian/Muslim merchants, who had been established on the China coast since the earliest days of Islam, who were responsible for introducing the cobalt blue to the Chinese potters at Jingdezhen. Indeed, analysis has shown that it was also Persian cobalt that was used to decorate Chinese *sancai* splashed wares in the Tang dynasty. The cobalt blue was probably exported in the form of glass smelt, to be ground down into pigment by the Chinese.

Apart from the use of the novel blue to decorate the porcelain, the other fundamental change was from the delicate small-scale wares of the Song dynasty to the massive heavily decorated bowls and dishes of the Yuan dynasty (1271–1368). This has been explained by the Mongol supremacy in the early fourteenth century, which linked China to Central Asia and the Near East under a single hegemony, and the importance of these early wares for export. One argument runs that the early blue-and-white was primarily an export ware, and reflects the taste of the Islamic market. This hardly squares with the inclusion of numerous Buddhist symbols in its decoration; and indeed the increasing number of early blue-and-white wares which are turning up in China itself. There are also the two most famous of all early pieces – the pair of vases now in the Percival David Foundation in London, dated AD 1356 and bearing an inscription dedicating them to a temple not far from Jingdhezhen.

When did all this take place? Although there are one or two odd, experimental pieces of blue-and-white about the turn of the century, it seems as if the real industry got going at the end of the first quarter of the fourteenth century, and we know from the David vases that it was fully fledged by 1356, with a complete repertoire of all the designs and motifs associated with this initial phase. There is further, if negative, evidence from a shipwreck off the Sinan coast of South Korea. This ship, laden in China with thousands of pieces of Chinese ware of all kinds and destined for Japan, sank according to wooden dockets also excavated from the seabed about AD 1323. And there was not a single piece of blue-and-white represented, although there is every other conceivable type of Chinese ware. This would suggest that when blue-and-white arrived, it arrived with a bang. The genius lies not only in the unequalled virtuosity of the painting, but the variety of design elements and their combinations.

Something should also be said about another contemporary ware, Chinese celadon. Celadon also has a stoneware base, but is light grey in colour rather than pure white. It is covered with a glaze ranging from grey-green to olive, under which the designs are carved and sometimes moulded; where the body is left unglazed, as it was often done on purpose, the iron impurities in the glaze fire to a subtle orange-red. Celadon was a development of the green wares in China, and like Yue stoneware the product of kilns to the east of Jingdezhen, in the Longquan district. It was also widely exported all over Asia and the Near East, and during the Yuan period and the early Ming dynasty mirrors in size and often design, parallel developments in blue-and-white. It has a subtle quality which has led to it never being as popular with collectors as the stunning blue-and-white, which by the sixteenth century seems to have virtually eclipsed it. It is also well represented in the Topkapi Sarayi collection, and at Ardebil. In many Persian and Turkish miniatures it features side by side with the blue-and-white, so it was certainly sought after as a royal tableware. There is indeed a legend that it was popular with Turkish Sultans because the presence of poison could be detected by a celadon plate. A Turkish lady museum director wrote recently about this that she had always wanted to test it, but that as, unfortunately, poison is not readily available these days, she had been thwarted!

Celadon also turned up in Syria in the seventies. One of the most interesting pieces was a broken celadon plate, which arrived in my office whilst I was teaching one day. I told my class to get on with it, and closeted in my office, I photographed the plate and drew its profile. What had caught my attention were six characters painted in black ink on the unglazed ring on its base. When read, these were indeed important, for they were a Chinese cyclical date, probably for 1384. As there are very few specifically dated pieces of celadon, this added one more, and I was able to persuade a Syrian collector to buy it. It is now sitting in his house in Aleppo. Another cache of celadon appeared with a dealer in Beirut, Farid Ziadeh. Farid lived in a magnificent four-storey old Lebanese house in Beirut – not far from Henri Pharaon – and I arranged to go and see his collection, again early one morning. I found I was not the only caller, for there were a number of black-robed Bedouin, straight from the Syrian desert. Farid engagingly told me that they were part of his network of runners, who would bring him antiquities from far and wide. He only sold wholesale, to the trade, which for him were Swiss or German dealers. He asked me what I was interested in, apart from Chinese pottery, as he was willing to make an exception for me. When I told him nothing, really, he was quite disappointed, for he said if he didn't actually have what I wanted in stock, he could have it made for me. He led me down the garden path to his atelier, where indeed a number of craftsmen were busy making antiquities of every sort. The Ziadehs ran a family business and his elderly father had the distinction of being the *doyenne des antiquaire.*

Quite apart from the celadon and blue-and-white which had remained in private houses and collections in Syria, Turkey, Persia and Egypt over the centuries, there is the archaeological evidence of its export from China. As the distinguished archaeologist Sir Mortimer Wheeler once observed, the usefulness of pottery is that it is easy to break but hard to destroy, and when broken pottery is found in a stratified archaeological context it is an excellent chronological indicator. Pottery of the same type can also provide a clue to cultural and commercial contacts over a wide area. Chinese wares are tangible evidence of this, and broken pottery and porcelain from the Far East has been found on a wide variety of sites. In the Near East, Chinese wares from at least as early as the Tang dynasty have been found in Iraq, at sites like the Abbasid capital at Samarra, and further south at Kufa. Quantities have also been found at the early Islamic site at Daybul, on the coast near Karachi, and also at the major port of Siraf on the east coast of the Persian Gulf. A sherd of Tang white ware was even excavated at Antioch on the Orontes, in Syria; and again it found its way as far north as Nishapur in Khorosan.

Perhaps the largest quantity of imported Chinese material has come from the rubbish heaps of Fustat, the site of old

Cairo on the Nile. This ranges from the Tang dynasty through the Song, Yuan and Ming, and there are literally heaps of broken porcelain, *qingpai*, Yue ware, celadon and blue-and-white. China has also been found right down the coast of East Africa, and the enigma of Zimbabwe, whose civilisation and date had been the cause of wild speculation, was finally solved in 1939, when the excavator, Gertrude Caton-Thompson, found a fifteenth-century Chinese blue-and-white bowl in a well stratified context. Chinese dishes and bowls were also built into the walls of mosques up and down the coast of Kenya and Tanganika. All this is obviously a sign of a vigorous maritime trade between the Far and Near East, ranging widely both in space and time.

The same is true for the Far East, and South-East Asia in particular. Much Chinese material has been found in Java and Sumatra, and Tom Harrisson found Chinese stoneware jars were popular heirlooms amongst the head-hunters of Borneo. In Vietnam, so-called Annamese wares clearly derive from Chinese prototypes. Again, in Malaysia and the Philippines Chinese porcelain is common, both surviving intact and also found on numerous sites in fragmentary form.

But what about the middle? As I became more and more intrigued with the Chinese porcelain found in Syria, the question posed itself – how did it get there? And if, as I speculated, it came by sea and then overland, there must also be evidence for its export in India, lying half way between the Near and Far East. Gradually a plan formulated itself in my head; if no one else had so far bothered to look for it systematically on the Indian subcontinent, then I would.

3

JOURNEY TO BOMBAY

IT WAS ABOUT THIS TIME that a chance encounter led to a happy turn in the development of my interest in the trade routes. I was teaching a class in sculpture at the American University of Beirut and a student enrolled whom I found difficult to place. He was obviously not an Arab, and with his fine dark features and curly black hair did not fit into any category I could think of. I asked him where he was from? He replied he came from the Maldive Islands. This sparked my interest, as I had been reading the account of one of the world's greatest travellers, Ibn Battuta, who was almost contemporary with Marco Polo, and who had travelled all the way from his native Morocco to China and back again. Like Marco Polo, he also described the remarkable pottery he saw being made in China in the early fourteenth century, and says it was exported all over China itself, to India and even as far afield as his own country. More to the point, Ibn Battuta spent a long time in the Maldives, on his way to the Far East. Inspired by this, when I saw my new Maldivian friend Hamid at the next class, I asked him more about the Maldives, and showed him a photograph of a piece of blue-and-white from Syria. Had he ever seen anything like it? 'Oh yes', he said 'we use Chinese dishes like this every Friday night, which is party night. We were all converted to Islam in the twelfth century, and after we have been to the mosque, we have a feast. Then we put all the dishes away again till next week. Incidentally, although we are Muslims, we are really pagan; you should hear some of the songs my grandmother used to sing to me!'.

However slight Hamid's account was, coupled with Ibn Battuta's detailed account of life in the Maldives, I was intrigued. The summer vacation was coming up, and I said to Peggy that instead of motoring to Europe, let's go the other way for a change, and try to get to India and the Maldives, in the quest for Chinese porcelain. We did not have much money, and as Kathy and Andy wanted to come too – Martha elected to stay with her father in Beirut – the Morgan seemed a sensible solution for at least as much of the journey that we could do by land. Initially we thought we would motor through Syria and Iraq to the Gulf, but it proved impossible to get an Iraqi transit visa in Beirut. So we decided to set off for Kuwait via Jordan and Saudi Arabia, and on 24 June 1974, we started from Beirut across the mountains of Lebanon.

Having an inkling that this was to be an epic journey, I began a diary. This was, I think, a means of keeping one's sanity in situations which became increasingly unpredictable. I should say that Peggy, Kathy and Andy all kept diaries too, Andy dictating his to his mother. Upon comparing them I was amazed to find that not only did all four differ in reactions to specific events, but that the events themselves were recorded differently. Andy, then aged seven, had to dictate his because he was handicapped that summer; answering a summons to class after morning recess at the Collège Protestant in Beirut, he had fallen out of a tree in the playground and broken his arm. This had been plastered up, and with his arm in a sling and his straight blond hair and generally waif-like appearance, he was particularly useful at frontier posts as evidence of the innocence of our trip. This role was later to drive him mad in the Maldives, where nobody had ever seen a blond boy before and people used to jeer at him and pinch his hair to see if it was real. One realised what it must have been like to be black in eighteenth-century European society. To defend himself we eventually bought him a water-pistol, which he used to great effect to repel the inquisitive.

Kathy, then aged sixteen, had her own adolescent cross to bear. She was also the object of much vicarious speculation, but managed to cope by adopting an almost constant air of disdain and hauteur. This crumbled slightly in the Maldives, where our aristocratic landlord, also aged sixteen, was married to a fourteen-year-old and had a twelve-year-old boy as their servant, and everybody reverted happily to childhood and spent endless hours playing snakes-and-ladders *à quatre*, and listening to Beatles records.

Peggy, apart from her role as co-driver, acted as general group mother and hostess, and spent much time calming all of us down when we had the inevitable fights due to too much close contact in the Morgan for too long, and came close to blows. Our first stop was at Shtaura, a little Lebanese town in the middle of the Bekaa Valley between the mountains of Lebanon and Syria. It is famous for its restaurants and shops full of smuggled goods, a great pilgrimage place for hungry Syrians after material delights unobtainable in their own country. It was a common sight to see them stuffing down garlic chicken and frogs legs preparatory to purchasing a fridge and arranging for it to be humped illegally over the hills and delivered in Damascus. We actually ate in a restaurant where I had had my first meal in the Arab world, in 1951, when I was travelling in a *service* taxi on my way to work as an archaeological draughtsman at Jericho, in Jordan.

Under a heavy load, for besides the four of us there was a quantity of luggage strapped on the back, Speedy Motor behaved well. By June it is already hot in the Near East, but that is alleviated to a certain extent in Syria where on the desert plateau the heat is dry, rather than humid as it was on the Lebanese coast. We got to Damascus late in the evening and were somewhat perplexed as they had once again changed the traffic system. We were turned down by two hotels before we found a third which would take us; Damascus was full of tourists, that is Gulf Arabs travelling in the opposite direction to ourselves to spend summer cooling off on the slopes of Lebanon. We spent a hot and airless night in a room opening onto a well, but luckily it was a short one as we were up at 5am and on our way. Light was smouldering across Chouhada Square as I fixed up Speedy for the day and injected the other three and all our baggage.

The way south through Syria on the main road to Jordan was one we knew well, and just outside the city there were lots of soldiers catching buses going in the same direction. One jokey bunch on the back of a lorry pretended to throw one of their comrades to us. We sped through Sheikh Meskin ('the mad sheikh') and past the turn off to Quneitra and the Golan heights; Mount Hermon had lost its icy cap. At Dera'a the Syrians waved us politely across the frontier. The Jordanian customs were less than welcoming, and we were taken in hand by a Tourist Policeman with a very red face, rather from the embarrassment of his job intervening on behalf of foreigners than from the scorching sun. First of all we had to drive onto a rack, so that we could be inspected from below. Then every single item of baggage had to be searched on a table. A silly soldier got distracted by Andy's toys and I got cross. There were innumerable moves in the game of passing through customs, filling in of forms and struggling to get our passports stamped. We got through at last, not without a lingering rancour, but this was soon dissipated after we had glasses of tea and the Jordanians were so friendly that unfortunately we forgot to pay for it. Quite soon, before Amman, we turned eastwards across the desert along the road to Baghdad, following the oil pipeline.

It began to get very hot, and we were stopped by a policeman, who looked wonderingly at a passport and said, 'Is this my mother?'. A nice idea, 'Take tea with us', he says firmly, I explained in my inept Arabic that we had just had some;

'Please speak Arabic slowly!' he retorted. What good advice. We continued across the crumbling desert, looking like Roman roads upended, of once neatly fitted black basalt slabs. When we arrived at H4, the Rest House there was also crumbling. But with visitors it came to life again; we rested hard for a few minutes. Andy meanwhile was outside, absorbed in a study of the inside of discarded bottle-caps. Quite shortly, we came to the H4 Customs, where a track leads off southwards for Saudi Arabia, for what we hoped would simply be a short swing across the desert to Turaif, where we would join the road again. There are conflicting stories of how long this should take, the general consensus being about two to four hours. A friendly lorry driver with fifty tons of Lebanese cement bound for Kuwait offered to guide us and carry all our luggage on his truck. This seemed like a good idea, but less so two hours later when he was still fiddling with his customs papers. His assistant suggested we could all sleep in the desert if we didn't make the crossing by nightfall. I began to cast around nervously and declared that it's all off unless we could leave within the next ten minutes. Eventually we set off, with less than three hours of daylight left.

Some hours later in the desert in the pitch dark we began to reflect on the folly of setting out so late. At sunset, the driver had insisted that we eat. He spread a blanket on the sand and opened a dusty locker in the side of his juggernaut, to reveal great slabs of ice on which were reposing peaches and plums, two sorts of melon, iced beer and fruit juices of all kinds, and twisted white cheese. We had a delicious feast followed by tea and coffee. We offered cigarettes, which were refused, and a lemon drop which the driver, Muhammad, took and after two sucks spat unselfconsciously far into the stony desert. Ahmad, the *walad* (boy), lit a stove behind a folding metal windbreak for the tea and coffee. We saw a magnificent sunset, and then set off in the dark, us lurching after the dusty truck in Speedy like a mad mouse. Later, we actually saw jerboas and a rabbit, dancing insanely in the headlights. The truck got a puncture in one of its sixteen wheels, the jack wouldn't work, and we ended up spending the night in the *sahra*, after all. Peggy, Kathy and Andy slept securely in the driver's cab. Muhammad, Ahmad and myself curled up on the cement on top of the trailer. It was clear, starry and surprisingly comfortable.

Next morning revealed nothing except a police fort miles away on the horizon, which the night before Ahmad had dismissed as a parked lorry. Ahmad ran about two miles at top speed to stop a passing truck, and missed it; he stayed there. We had a leisurely breakfast on the blanket, and Muhammad mended his jack; he had just finished repairing the gigantic wheel, when Ahmad and friends and trucks arrived from all directions. With much swearing and great good humour we set off again. Except that we didn't, because the car wouldn't start. We were towed away by our leader, so close to the rear end that all we could see was the dust the truck churned up. Blind, coughing and spluttering, unbelievably Speedy suddenly started. We then followed the truck at a more reasonable distance, with a second truck racing paternally along beside us. Apart from one great slide when we were stranded on a sandbank like a tortoise, we finally made it to Turaif.

All seemed to go well to begin with, but then the Saudi customs got nasty. They wanted to censor all the children's books, hypnotised by Kathy's girly magazine and her copy of the *Naked Ape*, which had a totally unrevealing but apparently for them overwhelmingly arousing picture of *homo sapiens* on the cover. This took hours. Finally we were rescued by Alfred, Tapline's (Trans Arabian Pipeline) man in Turaif, and he led us off to the comfort and cleanliness of the oil company's local canteen. Whilst the others rested in an air-conditioned room, I went to a garage in the *suq* and spent a cheerful afternoon having the car dismantled and washed inside and out. When it was cooler we set off again, down what must be the longest straight road in the Middle East, excellently surfaced, and running in tandem with the pipeline south-east across Arabia. At nightfall we arrived at Badrani, and after an encounter with some pushy Saudi soldiers who took it upon themselves to patrol all the pumping stations against incursions of saboteurs, and Scotch, we finally got inside and were allowed to camp rather forlornly on the grass.

All the Tapline stations are precisely the same in layout and the facilities they provide. This is very American, but it becomes rather peculiar, like a recurring dream, to visit them in sequence. The only variants are the position of the water-coolers, the height of the eucalyptus trees and the fertility of the grass. One man said it was all so similar that it became a game to try to dent the uniformity, rather like being in the army. But for us it was a passing phenomenon, for which we were grateful, but a little cross to discover that we could have used a private tarmac Tapline road from Jordan, thus avoiding the desert interlude. Also, that the Tapline executive in Beirut whom I had consulted before we set out, apart from omitting to tell us about the link road, had only instructed the stations along the road to mark our progress eastwards, so nobody knew quite how far company hospitality was to be extended. In the event I think we may have been given more than was intended.

We set off again at 5.30am just as the sun rose, on what was to be our longest day. It grew hotter, and hotter, and there was nothing to see, except the pipeline always with us on the right. It was sometimes flat on its belly, sometimes raised on trestles, and often making slight, awkward bends. We did pass lots of camels, young ones. We came to Rafah, which only confirmed its consistency with the other stations, and picked up fresh water. We stopped at lunchtime at Qaisumeh, where *Relations*, one Mohammed, was kind and put us in the guest house. We had air conditioning again, and lunch, and guiltily did some laundry which we strung up on our tow rope stretched between two trees; we slept. We made a tentative attempt to stay till it got dark, but it seemed we had overstretched our welcome. So we packed and left, only to find on leaving that we *had* been expected to stay.

It got even hotter as we edged further east and south. And dark, with the scrub turning a surprising bright green before the sun finally deserted us. We stopped at a road house and drank orange juice and tea by the light of a pressure lamp. No quantities of any liquid seemed to be enough for us. In the kitchen, rice and chicken were bubbling away. Outside, in a pool of light, men sat on high platforms, drinking tea and smoking *nargilehs*. I supposed that if one is used to sitting cross-legged at home, in such a cafe it is necessary to get everyone comfortably off the ground. There were a few chairs and tables for the more sophisticated.

We decided not to eat, but to drive the last two hundred and forty kilometres which would get us to the frontier. It was now so late that instead of taking one-hour turns driving, we divided the last stretch into sixty-kilometre slices. By now the road was bumpy, curved, and with a most erratic white line down the centre. Arriving at Khafji, we enquired about the Japanese petrol company station that was supposed to be there, but couldn't find it. A friendly Saudi passing by with his large wife directed us instead to a hotel. It had no name, and indeed didn't appear to have been recently occupied, although it bore traces of use long ago. Too tired to do more than rip the dirty covers off the pillows, we sank into the sordid sheets. Cockroaches waved their legs at us in the sumptuous imported marble Belgian bathroom.

We were up early for our final assault on Kuwait; breakfast was not bad, with eggs which were a cross between fried and scrambled, two sorts of jam, and tea. We piled all the luggage on the car again – how many times we were to perform this manoeuvre in the months to come. Mr. Al-Sirieh, the proprietor of the hotel, was a Saudi contractor from a village a thousand miles to the south. He explained to us that Khafji was operated by the Saudis and the Kuwaitis as a useful free zone, and was just getting off the ground.

On the road again, there was a fiendish hustle at the Saudi frontier. Many little windows in blank walls snapped open and shut, our passports were snatched and visas and the car indentified, and finally we were free to flee. I helped an Iranian working in Dubai and returning home to Tabriz to fill in his form, and chatted with a young American lad from San Francisco. He had hitched his way through Turkey and Syria to Jordan, and seriously wanted to know if the entire Arab world was queer. He had been propositioned by truck drivers so many times he was now only accepting rides from those wearing wedding rings. I told him this was just their sense of fun and had nothing to do with either marriage or morality; I hope I was right. Anyhow he didn't seem unduly phased; he told me he was on his way to Iran, then back through eastern Turkey to make his way along the Black Sea coast to Istanbul.

Across the frontier the Kuwaitis were light years better organised than the Saudis and everything went very fast. There was a final hot dash across a hundred kilometres of desert to Kuwait City, with only pylons and oil installations to relieve the landscape, although occasionally there was a glimpse of what might be a sheikhly pile out in the desert. I was reminded of a Beirut tale, of a Kuwaiti who had spent the summer in the mountains of Lebanon and became so enamoured of them that when he returned home he bulldozed up a little mountain of his own and pitched his tent on top. By this time, the sun was up and we were so dehydrated from the scorching hot air that we stopped at the first grocer's shop in town and drank every bottle of soft drink in sight, and burped our way onwards.

Kuwait was both bigger and lower than I had expected, with lots of good modern buildings and more older ones than I would have thought would have survived. There were mosques of all periods left stranded in wastelands of demolition. We went first to the shipping agent, for we had booked a passage for the car and ourselves onward to India before we had left Beirut. To our fury, we found the ship was now scheduled to leave two days later than we had been told, so we were stranded in Kuwait for three extra days, with little spare cash for this extra expense. A single hotel room with nothing else included cost us fifty pounds a day; but it was at least air conditioned and had a little fridge, so we stocked it up with food and drink, and our unexpected stay became quite tolerable. In the evening, although it was still hot, we went for a walk through the *suq*, and had *kousa mashih* – stuffed baby marrows – in a humble restaurant on an old square.

Although the next day was a Sunday, it was not a holiday and I busied myself with Speedy, going to various ministries and export offices to get an exit permit for it. I saw so many professional pleaders all dressed in white dishdashers I felt I was in hospital and we all ought to be in bed together. As the Indian sent by the shipping agent to guide me through the bureaucracy felt I also ought to see the fish market and various other unscheduled sights, this all took forever. We consolidated our new friendship with a Coke on the sidewalk. In the afternoon, back at the hotel we all slept, and in the evening drove out to the suburb of Salamieh. This was disappointing as there was nothing to be seen of the old port, and we ended up eating hamburgers rather than a hoped-for fish curry.

Next day was the first of July, and leaving the children asleep, Peggy and I got up early to visit the fish market. This was fascinating, for as we were to find later in the Maldives, although the fish were generally Mediterranean in style, they all seemed to be twenty times larger. There were gigantic shrimp for sale at only three pounds a kilo, so we bought some and took them to the restaurant where we had eaten the first night and asked them if they would cook them for us. I ended up cooking them myself with the help of the Iranian chef and a Palestinian waiter, and we took them back to the hotel for a picnic lunch in the bedroom, with lots of fresh fruit and a melon, drinks and iced water. I also managed to make coffee in the bathroom on my solid fuel stove. In the evening we had an Indian meal in the *suq*, with a chorus of protests from Peggy, who was appalled by the dirt and predicted dire results.

In the event we were fine, as indeed we were for the whole three months' trip. This was extraordinary, for we ate and slept in some of the most sordid accommodation in south Asia. Our good fortune was entirely due to a Lebanese doctor whom we had consulted at the American University of Beirut before we set out. He told us we should simply put a few drops of Chlorox (household bleach) in our drinking water. This we did, and I have always been curious to know if after this we ended up with twenty-two feet of spotless white intestines. The king-size bottle of bleach also came in useful in another way later on in the trip, which I will recount in its proper place.

At last, the day came to depart from Kuwait. We rose early and went off to photograph some of the mud-carved mosques in the morning light. Whilst the rest packed, I went off to see the Saudis and the Iraqis about possible transit visas for our return. At the Iraqi consulate there was an unpleasant Englishman bent on the same mission as myself, who when he found the right door to the consulate, shut it in my face. But I had my revenge, for the professional Arab filler-in of forms wouldn't touch his until he had leisurely done all four of ours. A French woman told me it takes about three weeks, but that the visas do eventually come. I then set off for the Saudi consulate, and found it in an extravagant pile beside the sea on the way to Salamieh. Visas were to be had from a tastefully decorated pale blue-and-white stucco shack on the left of the garden gate. After I had filled in all the forms, they were rejected by the official in charge and I was told to try again when we returned.

Back at the hotel we loaded up the car once more and set off for the port. We followed the plan of action mapped out for us by my Indian friend the day before, and the Port Director gave us tea and processed all our passports himself. We then scudded off across the sand searching for the boat, which we found, grey and slightly tilting, propped up against the quay. We correctly guessed that the next few days on the *Dwarka*, of British India Lines, would be quite a novel experience. In fact it took us eight days to sail to Bombay, down the Persian Gulf and across the northern Indian Ocean. We stopped but were not allowed ashore at Bahrain, Dubai and Muscat, although we had a morning in Doha and a day in Karachi.

It was the oddest voyage, for quite apart from the fifteen passengers like ourselves travelling cabin class, there were over seven hundred others on the deck. There were thus two completely segregated groups. The boat was old enough to be heavily fitted out in polished brass and mahogany, and the crew itself was in some kind of a time warp; half of the officers British and the other half Indian but more British than the British. We were trapped in a stultifying daily ritual of early morning tea, breakfast, luncheon, afternoon tea, drinks and dinner. The cabins were so tiny there was no escape and we were condemned to the public saloon. And the food; we were served kippers, steak and kidney pies, roly-poly puddings and porridge as we steamed across the Indian Ocean in the midsummer heat. Apart from the officers, whom we were told were all lucratively engaged in smuggling on the side, there were three American school teachers, two working in Kuwait and the third from New York. Two of them were gregarious, the third mostly silent and snide. There were also two schoolboys, flamboyantly rude, who fascinated Andy and took him in tow. The British Captain was grey-haired and jolly, and the nicest and most interesting of the lot.

It was Kathy who was astute enough to figure out that life below decks, or rather on deck, was much more fun. The deck passengers had sea breezes, whilst we stifled in our cabins. They also had delicious smelling curries cooked in large cauldrons, and on top of this, almost non-stop entertainment – Indian movies shown on a white sheet strung up between the masts. Nor were they poor; they were almost all working in the Gulf, and returning home laden with all sorts of consumer goods, fridges, TVs, ghetto-blasters and every kind of appliance, all piled up on the deck. Apart from getting excellent curry to eat, Kathy got locked in conversation with four hippies on their way to India, one American, one Persian, and two passengers from Beirut. In turn, she smuggled water and cans of beer down to them from our cabin class.

We went ashore at Doha, where there was little to do except wander round the *suq*. I bought a long white cotton dishdasher and a pair of striped drawers, and we also found some pretty baskets and a fan. I was intrigued to find the ship moored behind us was from the Maldives, our ultimate destination, and it was tempting to think that if it hadn't been for Speedy we could have trans-shipped direct. The next stop, Muscat, was entrancing, with the mountains rising behind the town capped by medieval forts, looking just as it does in William Daniells' watercolour of the same prospect. It also looked a little like Mukallah, half way along the southern shore of Arabia, which I had visited some years before; I was sad we could not go ashore to explore. The Captain told us that Beatrice de Cardi and two other British archaeologists had been there earlier in the year. In Karachi, we spent longer on land and hired a flashily-painted three-wheeled *jitney* in the market, to take us to the museum. Here we found some interesting fragments of both Islamic and Chinese pottery, mostly from the early Islamic port of Daybul. I interrupted the lady Curator in her office, in the middle of her curry lunch, to find out more. On board the *Dwarka* again, we learned from the radio that the monsoon had started with a vengeance, and Bombay had had its highest rainfall for a hundred and thirty seven years, and there were many drowned. Two days later when we finally arrived, lying offshore before disembarking, the city looked like the Thames Embankment on a normal foggy day.

4

INDIA TO SRI LANKA

WE LAY AROUND for hours until we edged into the port, and when we finally made contact with the dock, we still had to wait. At last we were ashore and struggled with our bags to the customs. I was sent off to deal with the car to the Customs House, an extraordinary Victorian pile with tons of torn-edged paperwork on three gigantic floors, rather like a sort of bureaucrats' Selfridges. I found myself in the annexe; two tries later, I found the right man. But it was now lunchtime, and anyhow I had been misled, for first I had to go to the agent. The agent was down the street, and had definitely gone off for lunch too, though many munched out of tin bowls at their desks; come back at 2. I returned to pick up the rest of the family and we found a room in a pistachio hotel of moderate class, at the end of a row which had the Taj and the Gateway to India at the other extremity. The Gateway to India had been built to celebrate the great Durbar in 1924, and overlooked the monsoon sea, which had an almost pinkish tone. There were grey steamers, old fashioned with single tall stacks, dotted around the bay, with low hills and grey skies in the distance.

The first impression of India was that it was different, definitely different to anywhere else. For a start, the terms of reference which one would apply to the Arab world, or

Europe, or the United States, simply had no bearing here, and this is surely what makes the Indian subcontinent so unique. The first impression of Bombay was of extravagance, with neo-Gothic and Romanesque buildings of amazing scale and elaboration. Set in deep green tropical shrubbery, the foliated Gothic seemed rather apt. But a later stage in the evolution of the city was quite unexpected, a plethora of twenties and thirties buildings equally lavish in style. They didn't go quite so well with the shrubs, and projected a sort of mouldy south coast seaside flavour. I learned later that a number of Jewish German architects had emigrated to India as a result of the pre-war exodus and they had been the source of the modernistic flats and cinemas.

Everywhere there were big black birds, flapping and cawing. There were also hordes of little black and yellow taxis, mercifully cheap, and red London buses. It was like South Kensington crossed with the tropical house at Kew, and everyone was wet, streaming from the frequent showers, clothes clinging to shiny black skin. After we had had a hot vegetarian lunch served in little tins on a big tray, I got back to the agent, to find everyone had gone home early because of the rain. We wandered aimlessly round the streets and saw all sorts of novelties, strange fruit and flower garlands, two little cows and a laundry. When we went out for dinner later, on one corner there was a shrine with young men hanging on to bells ringing beside a big cow model, with lots of incense, bright lights, mirrors and worshippers, which through the windows looked like a magic sitting-room. Dinner was a mistake, in a corner cafe with an English menu for Indian food and seventeen different sorts of ice cream. It gradually filled up with hippies in various transcendental states, who apparently wanted respite from oriental cuisine; it was a sort of Travellers Rest. Back in our room in the pistachio hotel, it began to rain down the open well on to which we looked, drowning the curry smells from three floors below. As the rain got heavier, it sounded like bullets snapping on a tin roof.

We woke and breakfasted at the dirty communal table of the hotel. Packed and ready to go, I set off to collect the car and Peggy shopped for plastic to protect us from the monsoon. It became clear that Speedy with its canvas top was perhaps not the most suitable of cars in that climate. The agents were just like the customs, with three more floors of paperwork, but more orderly as money was involved. They insisted that I only had a copy of the right document and although this is their mistake they made me buy a new ticket for the car back to Kuwait. Once more, I found myself back at the customs, padding after a wet sepoy, a gristled elderly man looking like a failed scoutmaster, along corridors of such length and up elevators of such a lingering pace that the only response was abject acceptance of one's fate. Again, lunchtime intervened, and we had a rendezvous at the ship for one–thirty.

The ship was now in the wilds of dockland, entered through the Red Gate. It was leaning towards the shore, amongst a forest of cranes, all failed, along the quay, where they appeared to have rooted like trees in the oily sludge years ago. Nobody had done anything about unloading the car. First one of the cranes had to be moved, for it was in the way of the operation of the ship's boom. A gang of workmen appeared armed with gigantic spanners, wrenches and hammers, and proceeded to pound at the crane's four legs. It was amazing to see it finally move inch by inch in the sludge, and grudgingly reveal a few feet of dock onto which the car could be set. At the same moment there was counter-activity in the ship; ropes were being leisurely moved and tarpaulins hauled back by the sailors, some familiar from the trip but careful to not look my way. The customs man was quite friendly though he made it clear he was here on a false errand, dressed up in oilskins and a sort of plastic Tibetan hat. It began to rain very hard, the crew on deck was washed out in seconds and the tarpaulin stretched once more across the open hold. Everyone was finished for the day, although it was only half past two. We made a date for ten o'clock the next morning; at this moment south India seems a very long way away.

Back at the hotel, we were barely able to reclaim our sordid room, as someone else wanted it. We went to the Prince of Wales Museum; it is very much like the V & A, even the style in which the more modern galleries are displayed. There was an incredible number of paintings, mostly from a private collection. Everything was bad, basically bad Italian but with a sprinkling of Charles Shannon and Wilson Steer. The Constable was so dark as to be indistinguishable, and the only good painting was a very pretty landscape by John Brett. If ever there was a climate unsuitable for oil paintings, this must be it; they were all in a shocking state, echoed by the peeling walls of the museum itself. Back in the hotel tempers finally snapped and we all had a flaming row about where to eat, and I didn't. We were all very tired.

Next morning I was back at the docks, waiting in the rain for the customs man. Speedy was ashore, rats had nested in the engine and the outside was covered with yellow splashes and betel stains; the mirror, car cover and screwdriver had all been stolen. But at the second try, it worked, and I cleaned up the car for an hour, the customs man still missing. In exasperation I took a taxi to his office; he was quite offhand – 'It was raining too hard', was his excuse. He still didn't want to come as it was now near his lunchtime; so he filled out the forms and 'examined' the car from a distance. I returned with the signed documents and attempted to pay the port dues. This took almost three hours in the cashier's office. At last, I got the car and drove off, only to find at the gate one form was missing. I now had a whole sheaf, one of which had thirteen stamps on it, each accompanied by comments and a signature. Everyone is hypnotised by detail, and they positively salivate over mistakes, particularly those made by their colleagues.

I finally got back to the hotel at five to three, Peggy and the rest having packed and waited since eleven. After a hurried snack we set off, fully laden in unbelievable sheets of rain, for Poona, feeling very vulnerable. We drove through Bombay and cut across to the mainland eastwards, past great blocks of tenements stranded in acres of flooded land. The countryside, like us, was wet and bedraggled, and gradually we climbed up into the hills. The road varied between fair and bad, but Speedy behaved fine. We considered stopping at two resorts marked on the map but missed both of them in the rain and continued on to Poona after all, arriving late at night. We found a modern hotel called the Shalimar, and the rooms had bolts inside and out, and very large padlocks on the doors instead of normal keys. The plumbing was an attempt to replicate bathroom fittings using no fittings except standard pipes and taps, and the result was rather satisfying.

Next morning the sun was shining and there was no trace of the previous day's weather. More odd, although we were in the middle of the monsoon season, we saw no more rain during the whole trip to the south. This may have been due to the fact that we aimed right down the centre of India, rather than sticking to the coast. We tried to make an early start, but Kathy was sick in her stomach and groaning quietly; we drove hard along very bad roads, got a puncture and had the spare mended at lunchtime for a mere two rupees. The countryside was very lush, with banyan trees and green fields freshly planted. The villages were full of thatched huts and from afar looked like the houses in Rembrandt's drawings. The road belongs to everyone and a lot of time is spent avoiding fatalities; lorries coming in the opposite direction bear straight down on you and you are *always* forced into the ditch. We saw a pack of monkeys by the road, and I stopped and followed them a little way with my camera. They scampered away across the rocks to the fields beyond, and one straggler got a sharp cuff from the leader of the pack when he finally caught up with the rest. Later, at lunchtime we saw a big black bear being led off on a long chain.

The women are always elegantly dressed whether working in the fields or road-mending. The men mostly wear shorts or an odd variety of clothes. For a great deal of driving we didn't seem to get very far. Although we caught tantalising glimpses of temple-tops in villages, we dared not stop. The flood waters in the river were a peculiar pale pink, and beside one torrent there was a great temple with steps leading down to the muddy water, into which hardy youths were diving. Although we meant to go at least another hundred kilometres, we got stranded in Belgaum. Even though we were staying there the hotel wouldn't change travellers cheques, and I had to ferret out the local bank manager at nine at night to get his authority for the hotel to accept £20. Peggy and I hired a tiny cab, rather like a carriage in a ghost train, and visited three mosques and a Jain temple. The first mosque appeared to have been converted from a temple, and I was led upstairs to hear the Qadi giving a sermon in Urdu. It was very impressive, and I could quite see how Ibn Battuta on his travels must have had a nice time circulating from one such gathering to another. As he would have known more about Islam than anyone else, he seems to have been always welcome; but one wonders in what language he communicated. Nobody I met spoke a word of modern Arabic, although my *salaam aleikum* brought a loud chorus of *aleikum salaams*.

The Jain temple was amazing. It was off the main bazaar, a square courtyard giving on to the first shrine, where a god sat in profile, dressed all in silver and with large flashing teeth, covered with flowers and gay decorations. Each new visitor leapt at a bell suspended above the god and clapped it, at which drummer boys rushed around in all directions. Behind, in a second shrine, there were more bells, this time of the sort you find on bicycles. There was a fat, half-naked attendant looking after a group of highly coloured wax images, with a sacred cow and more unidentifiable offerings. As we left a half-naked priest was organising the boys to process with a litter, upon which there was another reclining image, covered with flowers and something shiny. The rain thundered down, the bells rang out, and everyone rushed in all directions. They all seemed pleased that we were there, and there was no suggestion of hidden mysteries to be concealed. Back to the hotel in our tiny cab, the driver worked the windshield wiper by hand, as well as operating an ancient bugle car horn and driving with the other hand. It was a virtuoso performance, and when I asked him how much he wanted, he answered just like an Arab – whatever you wish, he said. I gave him twice as much as I thought I should.

We sped on south; although there was plenty to see, Kathy and Andy spent most of the time in the back sound asleep. Andy was still nursing his plaster cast, having broken his arm. Because we never knew where we would end up each night, or indeed what sort of adventures we would have each day, it was in some ways quite unnerving for the children and sleep was their way of switching off. Cooped up in the motor, we all got tired and edgy, and we usually ended up in frightful rows about something quite trivial, such as where to eat or where to stay. Luckily, at least the weather continued to be on our side. There was a cloud or two, but it was dry most of the way. Occasionally grey clouds scudding against white ones would produce a fast shower, but it never lasted very long. The landscape became quietly undulating, patches of scrub dissolving into villages of palms and tropical trees, with herds of cows and water buffaloes, thatched houses, children, men, women. I began to reflect how like south India was to Indian miniatures. Those miniatures, which I had always imagined to be highly stylised, in point of fact are almost photographic.

The roads were often lined with banyan trees, and the trees themselves full of monkeys, which often gathered in packs beside the road, with many little ones as well. Their faces were red, almost as if they had been hennaed, and their long tails perfectly balanced every movement. They were quizzically concerned with everything passing by, wanting perhaps to be part of the action. All the lorries continued to head straight at us; I tried once or twice to keep my nerve, but every time I was forced into the gutter. But, curiously, we only saw one accident during the whole of our drive, and that because of the exceptionally muddy conditions on a culvert. We stopped to buy a picnic; I found bread, sliced and neatly tied up in a newspaper with purple thread and some mixed biscuits. I asked a grocer for cheese, or fish; he cackled dryly in disbelief at such a request. I collected four guavas, four mangoes and four apples for four rupees from a street stand – a lot. I found three soft drinks and a bottle of beer in another shop. Each time we stopped, the car was submerged within seconds with clusters of men and boys. One old man even thrust his grandson through the window so he could have a closer look at the spectacle inside. But they were easily shooed away, and once we started the crowd parted like the Red Sea. We had our picnic by the roadside; away in the distance a man wrestled with his plough on the edge of an immense field; two boys edged along the side of a tropical copse with a bicycle; and we were circled as we sat by a mangy, beaten dog.

As we drove on, the people seemed to be blacker, with an almost blue sheen. As we bounced south through the state of Mysore, the dress seemed more formal; in one village, three men in turbans with appliquéd coats of many colours looked just like the Magi. Later in the afternoon we stopped by a temple, and walked into an enclosed area of tumbled stones. Old graves grew out of rocks. The temple, four-square and indeterminate in style on the outside, was almost Islamic inside in its transition from square chamber to dome above by the use of squinches. In the centre two youths attended the shrine, where a cloth-covered sarcophagus was held down by stones at the corners and covered with strings of tiny flowers. Above, the rosettes carved in the centre of each stone panel seemed almost classical, and indeed apart from the recent application of silver paint to some of the finials, the dark brown temple had a distinctly classical feel. On the other side of the courtyard was a second open whitewashed temple with what almost seemed to be a *mihrab*. All the time we were there, perhaps only ten minutes, the wind howled through the temple enclosure. As I put on my shoes to leave, the nearest youth ran up to me with a newspaper packet. I gave him a rupee for the temple, and when I opened the packet in the car I found it was full of dried flowers, dirty sugar and seeds.

The land grew more bare, and occasionally there were ponds full of pale magenta water lilies. We passed a maroon-coloured stone lintel still supported by two posts carved with elephants, and further on three carved figures propped up insouciantly in a field by the road. The car bumped along fast, like a shaky ship on a choppy sea. Boats in Ibn Battuta's time were stitched together with coconut fibre for resilience – perhaps a Morgan would be better for it too. Finally, we arrived in Bangalore, after passing through mountains with the stones and rocks whitened at the edges, all half-round and never completely three dimensional, just like the rocks in Indian miniatures. I also noticed how faithful is the suffusion of green in Indian painting to nature. Green tree snakes, like green leaves; green saris, green fields; it was not at all the dried up landscape that I had imagined south India to be. Arriving late in the urban sprawl of Bangalore it made no sense; we stayed in a crumbling house in a crumbling garden.

But I don't think we ever did see Bangalore properly, for we were in a sort of Wimbledon Common area, with nineteenth-century mansions, gardens parks and palaces. The main street, like Edinburgh, was one-sided with the shops facing a park opposite. The shops themselves were rambling and indifferent, with a sprinkling of bars and coffee houses between the emporiums. Everything we wanted was close at hand, supermarkets, post office, bank, petrol and Automobile Club. Setting off again we made a detour to see some famous falls, still hoping to make Madurai the next day. We passed through a temple town, with a shrine in tiers on a high hill and a staircase leading up to it. At the bottom was a tank with steps leading down into it and many displaced carvings, a double elephant doorway and a cobra shrine. The houses were mostly tiled, and in another nearby town which also had many temples the shops in the main street were all set in classical stone houses with carved lintels, perhaps as old as the temples themselves. To crown it all, there was a fine painted statue of Mr. Gandhi at the entrance to the town.

We left the main road to Madras, into increasingly bumpy countryside and village after village of Tamil peasants. It was a rich countryside, wooded and full of flourishing crops. The villages were humming with activity. The people are slight and short and very black, but with delicate features. The blackness is only emphasised by the whiteness and general cleanliness of everyone's clothes, shirts and saris alike. A great store seems to be set on cleanliness, and on top of this everything appeared to be nicely ironed. I felt very slovenly; was it only tourists like us who hop around in dirty gear? There were lots of interesting things going on in the villages, making hand-built pots, constructing houses with the corner poles and thatched roofs first and then filled in with mud-bricks, chipping basalt for grinding stones, besides all the more usual activities such as planting rice, ploughing with buffaloes, drawing water, driving cows, knocking down cashew nuts, washing animals and cleaning clothes.

The falls we were aiming at were in wilder country, and we dropped down through purple-brown rocks and clusters of jungle outcrop in the valleys. The road closed in with trees and thorny scrub; shortly after we passed a fakir, two spotted deer leaped across the road. At the bottom we came to a clearing, with a village of thatched huts and a new Tamil Nadu Tourist Hotel with a bar. Everyone was very friendly and welcoming but there were mutterings amongst us about the cleanliness of the kitchen, which I objected to as a topic in front of the staff concerned. We parked the car and left for a sullen picnic on a stony hill beside a crumbling temple.

The temple was decorated with tiers of stucco over a brick base and crumbling away. Animals had been inside leaving dusty prints, and to the left of centre was a sacred stone cow in the inner shadows. Outside the temple was a raised square with a well-polished sunken *lingam*. Below, the river was in flood, a muddy torrent clattering over the rocks, and the smoke from a waterfall rose amongst the rocky islets. Later on we went for a walk to the falls, where there was a circle of little cafes amongst the trees for teas and soft drinks, soap and brown cigarettes. Also in the trees were two painted idols facing each other, with broken coconut shells before them; I had noticed this at our picnic temple, too. And there were monkeys, and big round baskets black with pitch on the outside, which turned out to be boats.

A path led across to the falls, where ladies in various stages of undress were washing, and as near as we could get to the water a fat man in a loin cloth was being given a good wash and rubbed down with oil. We left this greasy spectacle and retreated back along the path. Two monkeys plopped out of a tall tree on one of the islands and swum vigorously against the current to the mainland; I had never seen a monkey swim before, nor indeed a wet one. We paused for drinks and then climbed down below the falls to the river bend, where there was a great sandy strand which to Peggy's delight was full of delicate little conch shells. I climbed a rock, and saw the falls, smoking in the distance between craggy points; it was very like looking at Marcel Duchamp's mysterious waterfall in the Philadelphia Museum. Below, a fisherman asleep under his round basket boat was woken up by others who wished to pole across the river. Two men were cast off to fish with ring nets from one of these coracles, which was quickly carried away downstream by the current.

At the far end of the strand was a great crowd, set against the bed of the muddy river with a backdrop of scrubby hills and chasing clouds. It was, apparently, a film being made, and a young man ran across the strand with extra reels of film stock. On the way back to the hotel we were overtaken by two buxom starlets, one skirted and one in pants, both with large bosoms and many sequins. They were followed by a train of bemused Tamils. Earlier, two intelligent monkeys had associated Andy with bananas after he had fed them a bite of one, and got into his seat in the back of the parked car. They had found the packet of bananas on the front seat, and had just peeled and eaten one when I chased them out, one of them still with a banana sticking out of its mouth in a very rude way. This still did not prevent it hissing at me in a provocative and indignant manner. There were more monkeys around than necessary, and I began to feel that they lose their charm when seen en masse.

Back in the hotel we went to see our dinner cooked. The kitchen had a range of raised fires, each with flaming staves of wood inserted under the pots. The fish fillets were river fish, *kupti*, dipped in marsala, a peppery sauce, and deep fried. The sauce is a mixture of cumin, pepper, poppy seeds and coconut. To one side was a basalt roller and a quern, and near it a basket full of *puri* dough and little *puri* cakes, just about to be patted out thin for baking. The dough was under a cover of plaited leaves. On one side were the shiny dishes for our vegetable condiments. For dinner, there was the full works for the 'most famous film star in India-Tamil', the star of more than seventy films. We got fried fish and *puri* served on plates, with knives and forks. The film star kissed his wife and little daughter, and a funny white dog danced around. The starlet was, reputedly, waiting for him in his room. Across the corridor was a room full of large black men in white cotton robes sitting on the beds with long guns; these were hunters going out to shoot the next day.

We climbed out of the valley next morning, leaving the film stars behind for another day's hard work. They were being made up on a balcony, overlooking the monkeys. One fat character had flashing white teeth, regular eyebrows and an Adolph Hitler moustache, and a bright orange mouth. He watched us pensively as we loaded up the car. We turned south at the first village and drove through an idyllic succession of Tamil villages and villagers. The men were naked except for loin cloths and the women dressed in green saris, the colour of the land itself. Again, everyone was busy with rural tasks; the land seemed exceptionally rich, with all the necessary animals to complement it. In the morning light it took on a dream-like quality. This was only broken when the road disintegrated, and we had to edge the car gingerly through a shallow river, full of stepping-stones. We only just made it up the rutted bank.

One town we passed had a great fortress crowning a slumbering rock, and an ancient wooden juggernaut below by the roadside with a dusty covering of plaited palms. Here we bought fruit, a pineapple, bananas and sour but delicious oranges. In the next town we bought bags, roughly printed with elephants and goddesses and Tamil advertisements. I tried to take a picture of two pairs of brass-mounted bullock horns, in the middle of a gigantic crowd blocking our car and all the other traffic. I lost my wallet, but luckily there wasn't much in it.

Back on the main road we did not make very fast time to Madurai. Here the great temple rose out of the frequent showers. It was ominously oppressive seen across the river bed under a black sky. After we had settled in a government rest house, we set out to see it. It was gigantic and mostly hideous; you entered through a colonnaded passage, filled with shops selling all sorts of souvenirs, toys and garlands of flowers. We had already cast off our shoes and got a metal tag in return. There were thousands and thousands of pilgrims everywhere, running from shrine to shrine, putting hands reverently together and passing on, clapping the odd bell here and there. We paused alongside one of the galleries above the great tank; it was full of white-clad men, reclining before the muddy water. On the walls there were the deteriorating remains of mural paintings, in strip-cartoon fashion. But almost everything, including the towering sculptured pyramids, had been recently and hideously repainted, the total effect like Disneyland, a sort of Hindu theme park. But then individual shrines, enclosing indistinguishable oily statues that had been pelted with flowers and offerings, were full of mystery. So was a man in the shadows, sitting cross-legged in a Yoga trance, toes tucked under and staring into infinity. And there were *lingams* inlaid with what looked like a large piece of almond, with a prow to one side. We could not see into the inner shrines except by occasional glimpses through the entrances. We passed dark cages full of green parrots, and stalls selling bananas and other fruit neatly packaged in palm fronds. The whole sensation, in the darker parts, was like Persepolis come to life and complete. Night time was a good time to be there.

We walked back very tired, and dined in a restaurant called the Taj on their dirty 'roof', off saffron rice with some mildly hot but scanty pieces of mutton, buried in the mound.

Next morning we sped off to Mandapam, after cleaning Speedy Motor. First we stopped at the Mariannam tank, where a pretty temple normally floats in the centre of the great reservoir. The tank was dry, but the even grass on the bottom had taken its place and gave a similar effect, except there was no reflection and the grazing cattle appeared to be walking on water. A little girl posed herself for a photograph; Andy was added to the composition and rather spoiled it.

The road onwards was slow and it was very hot. The land became more desert-like, with thorn trees spreading horizontally and dusty scrub. Amongst all this we came across a gaily painted group of statues, with an outsize horse and rider, and snake charmers and other figures grouped around. Besides these there were two older, black and glistening and beflowered warriors with weapons raised in anger, and at right angles to them three more oily black statues. The annointing serves to make the black stone figures look like the sweaty black-skinned Tamils. It also makes it very hard for the eye to understand the form, the difference between painting sculpture with a glossy, rather than a matt, finish.

At Mandapam we found the railway station lost among a clutch of dark thatched cafes, surrounded by huts where carpets of silvery fish lay drying in the sun on coconut mats. We arranged to load the car onto the train at two o'clock – for thus we had to get to the ferry – and looked for a fish lunch. This we found, not surprisingly, in the Government Fishing Research Rest House, where they took pity on us, and served cutlets with marsala dressing, salads and larger slashed pieces of a fried fish tasting rather like mackerel. Afterwards we loaded ourselves and the car on to the train for the ride from the peninsula to the island of Rameswaram. Almost all the other passengers were Hindus on pilgrimage to the temple there, at this moment in the middle of a ten-day festival. The train ran slowly across the sea, here a pale emerald colour with a fast eastbound current, against which were struggling millions of tiny silver fish. As you could not see the track beneath, or anything of the supporting structure, it was almost as if the train was being levitated to the holy island, just a few metres above the water. Under the water you could also see the remains of an ancient causeway. The island was much bigger than we had anticipated. The train stopped at Rameswaram, although until ten years ago it had continued to Danuskhodi on the southern tip. A hurricane had destroyed the port and all the houses, and a train with three hundred students on it, of which only the empty engine was left. Abandoned, Danuskhodi's function had been replaced by Rameswaram, which also catered for the thousands of pilgrims who came to worship at the temple.

We arrived at a bad moment, particularly as we had to wait a couple of hours whilst the car could be shunted around to the unloading ramp. All the hotels were full, and the agents for the ferry to Sri Lanka tried to find somewhere for us to sleep. I set off with one of them in Speedy and got caught up in a procession headed by an elephant, giant dancing figures and a great silver peacock followed by a golden lion, drums and pipes and many Brahmins. It should be said, however, that Speedy created quite a stir too. Every night for ten nights this procession went to a different house, and this night it was to a house just opposite the agent's office. We saw the procession, but there was still no room available anywhere. So the agent took pity on us, and we drove out of town through great sand dunes anchored with palm trees to a shady garden with a thatched hut. It was an ice-making plant temporarily in disrepair. We slept on the concrete floor of the hut; the stars seemed very close above, and everyone was very friendly.

We woke very stiff and packed up and went back to the town to the agent's office. We started the 'paperwork', and I was asked if I could help with a truck belonging to the company, full of ice from another factory, which had broken down five miles north of town. We drove out with a spare wheel, to find the truck collapsed exactly at the end of the tarmac road, half the ice unloaded and melting fast into the hot sand. They unloaded the rest of the cargo and changed the wheel, with much heaving of limbs and disorder of dress, the driver inadvertently revealing a magnificent pair of balls. On the way back we passed several ruined temples, with an almost Greek aspect. And back in Rameswaram the shops and houses appeared to be set in much older structures, with columned porticos. One had beautifully carved impost blocks, and a doorway to match. There were *choultries*, pilgrim-hostels, everywhere; one would not have been out of place on the Grand Canal in Venice, its facade in best Renaissance style. Another *choultry* in classical manner, with two colonnades along the front and carved elephants at either end was worthy of an Irish baronet.

Our papers ready, we drove down to the port, scattering native babies to left and right into the shadows of their palm huts. We went through the ritual of leaving India, as complicated but not quite as bad as arriving, and all conducted with very good humour thanks to the agents, who were three very charming Muslim brothers, with a large and clever staff. The car was driven on to the sand and up a series of inclined planks on to two old boats lashed together. Here Speedy sat amidships, waiting to be towed out with us in another old boat, to the ferry waiting out at sea. The ship, Glasgow-built forty years ago and full of brass fittings, was in *Dwarka* style but better. It had once belonged, with another vessel, to Indian Railways, but now sailed alone back and forth to Sri Lanka twice a week, except for two months in the winter when it went to Bombay for an overhaul. The Third Engineer told me he had worked on ships all over the world, but now had only five more years to go and had gravitated to this easy run. The ship sailed full in the other direction, with eight hundred passengers on every return journey – all displaced Indians rejected by Sri Lanka.

We had a quiet voyage, we had tea and biscuits in the little lounge and sat up on the deck. There were quite a few young people, mostly French, also crossing to Ceylon. Speedy sat proudly on the bows. During the trip, we had time to read a guide book we had picked up:

Guide to Rameswararn, Cape Comorin, Tiruchendur, Courtallam

by T. J. Rajagopalam

Sri Karthikeiya Publications,
28 Jadamuni Koil Western Street, Madurai.

It included these facts:

KODAIKANAL

Sembaganur Post Office:
This post office became famous in 1947 for being the tidiest post office in India. The tidiness is seen even today.

Pillar Rocks
These rocks are three imposing bounders, about 400ft. in height, behind which are steady places for picnics and below these bounders are several caves and chasms.

5

SRI LANKA

WE ARRIVED as it was almost dark at the end of a wooden jetty. On land we could just see an endless belt of coconut palms and a narrow, sandy strand. Talaimannar consisted of a fishing village, a collection of bottle-shops and the meagre railway station. We set off in the dark hoping to get at least as far as Mannar, twenty-five miles south on the tip of this narrow island, stretching out like a finger towards India. In fact, India is joined to Sri Lanka by a chain of underwater reefs, which makes it impossible for a vessel of any size to sail between the two. This fact is known to any sailor but few scholars, and I have seen innumerable charts of world trade routes in academic publications demonstrating the impossible. The ferry, for instance, sailed along the eastern board of these reefs, which are known variously as Adam's Bridge, or Rama's Bridge. However, there are narrow channels both on the Indian side (which we had crossed over in the train) and also south of Mannar, which allow lighter craft to pass back and forth.

In the dark, the jungle looked fearsome, but every few yards we would pass a peasant walking home, often with an electric torch. Mannar, at the end of the causeway, was fairly unprepossessing, but we found the rest house on the outskirts of the little town and had a curious supper of steak and pineapple, following the example of two close-cropped young Swiss, male and female, looking so strange and peculiar in Sri Lanka. They were having a meal before retiring to their camper, which was parked in the garden under a banyan tree. We had a very hot, sweaty night, with all four of us on two narrow beds inside a pink peeling room. Outside the wind howled and it looked like the monsoon, but it died down before dawn.

It was so hot and I had sweated so much I thought I had a fever. But everyone else felt the same. Before breakfast, alerted by an extraordinarily well-informed petrol pump attendant across the road from the rest house, I visited the old Dutch fort a few yards down the road. A chatty soldier showed me round, and thanks to him we had a guided tour. At that moment it served both as a prison and also as a defence against any attacking Indians. Previously, I had been all round the outside of the fort, and where a muddy pond had partly eroded the debris at the foot of the wall, I found a quantity of seventeenth-century Chinese blue-and-white sherds. Inside, where a latrine had been dug, there were fragments of later eighteenth-century porcelain.

We had another conversation with the petrol pump attendant, who did seem to be quite impressively well informed. When he asked me what I was up to and I outlined my reasons for travelling to India and the Maldives, and my interest in trade, he told me that I should then go and visit Tirukeetheswaram, an ancient site a few miles away. This was Mantai; little did I know that I myself would excavate the site a few years later. And later we also learned why he was so well informed; he didn't just attend the petrol pump, he owned it, and was also the leader of the important Muslim community in Mannar. He had actually just finished his degree in history at Peredeniya University, and I think he rather enjoyed confounding me with his detailed knowledge. Our chance encounter was to have significant consequences, and Mohammed Farouk later played an important role in our lives.

To get to the site we had to cross the causeway from Mannar to the mainland, and then turn left for about five miles across the salty marshes. Here there was a large pond and a small village, and a Hindu temple in the style of Rameswaram. All around the temple was a dried-up double moat, and various hillocks and signs of excavation. This was all that remained on the surface of the kingdom of Mantota, ancient Mantai, which lasted till the ninth century AD. As we searched for sherds, and picked up some turquoise glazed and irridescent Islamic fragments, two young men bounded up with shouts of welcome. They had previously accosted Kathy, who was bored with our search and had stayed in the car, and put the wind up her. They were actually two young archaeologists and they took us to their dig, which was a very large uneven pit at the centre of the jungle-covered site, and a smaller deep hole with very straight sides and nothing much else. From the section it appeared quite baffling, as it seemed to be ten metres of earth and pottery mixed, with no walls or stratification at all. But perhaps it was the weathering on the side of the trench. They had found nine pieces of carved grey stone, which they thought might be a Sanscrit inscription. It was actually foliated *kufic*, and the piece they showed us was part of an Islamic tombstone. We photographed it, which was just as well as it disappeared without trace and we were never able to find it again; Nor could we ever locate the other eight pieces, which they had sent to Colombo. But this fragment was evidence of the occupation of the site in the Islamic period. There were also quantities of material from the other direction, sherds of celadon (actually Yue ware) and parts of bowls splashed with green decoration. We decided we would have a closer look on our return.

We set off inland for Colombo, expecting the road to rise, which it didn't. For a while the landscape looked like the English countryside, then there would be a cluster of tropical vegetation, or a pond of water lilies, bright pink and huge, and a kind of water hyacinth. The people looked like the Tamils in south India, but the women more often dressed in skirts and blouses rather than saris; the closer to the capital we got the more demure they became. We passed lots of churches of different periods and styles, suggesting a strong Christian presence. At a village by the sea, we wanted to eat fish, but there was no restaurant. Tantalisingly, in the market there was a great blue lobster in a tin of water, and shrimps and crabs and all sorts of other fish, but nowhere we could see to cook them. So for a rupee I bought a pineapple instead, and we stopped in front of a little Christian church to eat it. This episode was spoiled by being attacked by flights of hungry, vulturous crows, who turned out to be keen on pineapple, too.

By lunchtime we had got to another town, and in a peeling rest house similar to the one we had stayed in the previous night, they went and bought crabs for us in the market. But they were sad crabs, too warm from cooking and crying out for mayonnaise or some sort of sauce. The shrimps were fried in batter in sweet, buttery coconut oil and had a very strange taste. The bill was enormous, and left us all cross. I wanted to stay, but Peggy wanted to go on, and so we drove to Colombo at top speed and arrived well after dark. Lots of the street lights were out, and we drove round for hours and hours trying to find somewhere to stay in our price range. At last, I put my trousers on – I was wearing filthy shorts – and stalked in to the Samudra; this was a hotel school, in what used to be a smart colonial Colombo club, next to the racecourse. We got in, exhausted.

Culinary interlude:

THE CEYLON OBSERVER

Economical dishes with left-overs

TOAD IN THE MOLE
Ingredients: Any Left-over.

Having decided it was too expensive and instead of deserting the Samudra, the Samudra deserted us. I woke up to angry noises outside the window (we were on the ground floor) to see soldiers and servants in animated conversation. The young man at the reception told me the police had arrived before the staff, to tell them they didn't have jobs any more. As far as I could gather, the Samudra had passed from the Department of Tourism to municipal administration, and in the process the municipality had decided to shed the staff and replace them with their own. This left the clerk and one servant inside, and the rest locked out. But surprisingly, breakfast appeared, behind closed shutters.

We went to the post office and found letters waiting for us, changed money and discovered what the area we had circled around last night really looked like. It was quite different; I later learned that last night's unnatural darkness was partly due to the fact that Colombo had run out of electric light bulbs, for lack of hard currency. Thinking ahead, I tried to ring the Maldivian Consulate, but there was no reply; and as it was Saturday we resigned ourselves to doing nothing serious until after the weekend. Colombo on a Saturday was shut tight, shops and all, and resembled a Sunday in the west. Sunday turned out to be a sort of double-Sunday.

We had lunch in a Chinese restaurant, the Nanking, the first of many we were to have there; it was good, and cheap, and full of assorted travellers and lowheeled locals. We tried to see the museum – shut again – and went off instead to the zoo. This was excellent, small enough to be not too exhausting and numbered like a treasure hunt so you saw everything without having to try and remember what you hadn't seen.

Everything seemed to be in threes, particularly the birds; one wondered if the trio included a spare, sort of like a light bulb. The tropical landscape made a great setting and the animals didn't look half as sad as they do in London. There was a Syrian bear, *Ursus Syrianus*, called Soraya, and a very large gorilla with a little mate. There were also lions, leopards, monkeys and snakes; but the main attraction seemed to be a pair of white English swans.

In the evening we walked round the fort in the downtown section of Colombo, and found a shop still open. It was full of gems in front, but behind were hundreds of Chinese transfer plates and a lot of Korean pottery with dull blue designs that looked as if they had been done with potato cuts; some of these have turned up in Damascus too. What I first took to be bulbous watch-cases were in fact betel boxes, and there were rectangular brass tobacco containers of the Dutch period. There were masses of Victorian jewellery, often with missing stones, but very pretty. I was very taken with a cheese dish and a Japanese inkwell with three compartments marked 'Black', 'Red', and 'Copying'.

Whatever you can say about Sri Lanka, it certainly isn't India. Whether it is because it is a relatively isolated island (rather like Great Britain), or whether it is because of its history of colonialism, looking both to the east and west as well as the subcontinent, it has a very distinct personality. Admittedly on our first visit the rumbles of civil war were still faint, but there was a kind of underlying tension. And as I was to find out, this was no new phenomenon; for a thousand years, since the Chola invasions and the rape of the land, the epicentre had moved south from the ancient capital at Anuradhapura. Colombo developed as a capital city, with the Portuguese, Dutch and British as colonial powers, each for almost exactly a hundred years. The British favoured the Tamil minority, as much for their professional skills as anything else, rather as they encouraged the Copts in Egypt. When independence came, the Sinhalese managed to eliminate the Tamils from positions of power in the bureaucracy, so they became increasingly isolated in the north, centred on the Jaffna peninsular. Coming as we did from Beirut, where the civil war had actually begun, it seemed a blessed relief to be in a land where everyone smiled, stuck flowers in their hair, and seemed so universally good natured and intelligent. And yet horrors so unspeakable, even in Beirut terms, were just around the corner; we were lucky to have seen it before the abyss.

Colombo itself is not without charm; it stretches for miles from the fort – and the port – in the north, with the street markets of Pettah and the main commercial centre, to the open green space of Galle Face, and then Galle Road following the coast all the way to the southern suburbs. Galle Face is the public playground, facing out to sea; everyone promenades up and down the shore, and hundreds of kites swerve up and down, making the most of the strong sea breeze. Impromtu games of cricket, football and whatever constantly assemble and dissolve. It is all very gay and animated; and yet I have never felt lonelier than sitting on the grass, staring out to sea. Perhaps because one is aware of how far that ocean stretches, all the way to Africa, that induces a feeling I have never had anywhere else, of truly being at the end of the world. I have never, for instance, experienced anything like it in India, which is a far vaster country. There is a strong element of introspection in the Sri Lankan character as well; it is desperately important to succeed, especially for the young, and the passing of examinations assumes a disproportionate amount of attention. Failure often ends in suicide, or at the very least deep depression. Leonard Wolff captured this pessimistic mood perfectly in his first novel, *A Village in the Jungle*, and his analysis of what he saw when he was a young and inexperienced commissioner in the north is finely described in the first part of his autobiography. When I began to get deeper into my own research in Sri Lanka, trying to fathom out its complex history and relationships with the outside world, I could see how much of all this came about, but there still remains to this day, for me, some inexplicable factor.

We were, after all, at this stage simply tourists, and anyhow on our way to somewhere else, the Maldives. Again, it was not till later that I realised that the key to what I sought was in Sri Lanka, not there. In the meanwhile, we decided to make as much of our short stay as possible, within the limits of our time and money; we did, however, still have Speedy Motor. We spent a day going to Kandy and back; it was about seventy miles away, 1800 ft. up in the hills. After the suburbs of Colombo we finally began to wind through a succession of villages. So many people were using the roads just for walking that it made driving very slow, but the scenery was very pretty. Just as the guidebook said we would, we saw a working elephant; the villages were perched among bright green paddy fields, surrounded by clumps of coconuts and all sorts of tropical plants and flowers. It was a grey day with a lot of cloud, but once I saw a tiny patch of Tiepolo blue sky. The main monsoon was over, but Sri Lanka always seems to be hot and humid; indeed it was a local joke that it always rains more in the inter-monsoon period, between the two annual monsoons! I was to also discover that the monsoons make for bad archaeology, or at least for very complicated stratigraphy. First of all, each year the typical wattle and mud structures meld, and when they disintegrate they disappear seemlessly into the earth. This makes the disentangling of the remains of these domestic structures incredibly difficult. Secondly, the humidity means that there is an almost complete absence of the remains of anything of organic origin – silk, paper, textiles, wood and all sorts of goods mentioned as having been traded; even metal becomes corroded. What is left? Well, pottery for one, glass and quartz, and gold. But these alone give an incredibly unbalanced picture of society. One is, of course, on safer ground dealing with stone structures, carving and inscriptions. But it is a far cry from the Near East, and the almost 100 per cent preservation of material that you find in Egypt. Added to which Sri Lanka is in the cyclone belt, and any site stands the chance of being violently churned up.

Kandy, the historic medieval capital, was rather a let down; maybe it was that Sunday spirit again. There was the Queens Hotel and lots of tawdry, shut shops of no great note. The lake looked like a mere suburban pond, with villas around it to match. We searched for a schoolmaster friend of Hamid's, to whom he had given us an introduction before we left Beirut. We found him at Trinity College, the leading establishment for the upbringing of Sri Lankan youths, at his home on a hill top, with his fat wife. Their lunch was on the table so we did not stay long, for which they were visibly glad. We had ours in something called the Bake House; it was awful, half of it didn't arrive and the rest of it we wished hadn't. As Kandy is the sacred seat of Buddha's Tooth, I was prompted to reflect how he might have lost it.

We saw the museum, which had interesting bits and pieces from palace life of the Kings of Kandy; I was intrigued by some ewers of uncertain date, but of the type which are seen on fifteenth-century Syrian tiles, for which no prototypes are known. We got into the side entrance of the temple; it was the wrong time of day to see the tooth, but we saw the outside of the shrine, also supposedly fifteenth century, with nine ladies on the ceiling forming an elephant in an Archimboldo sort of way, with lots of sexy rabbits and pairs of warriors locked in love, or combat. Upstairs, on a higher level, there were pilgrims, mostly women and children, carefully placing their offerings of flowers on a table before the shrine, after having first freshened them up in the fountain below. The table was a bed of flowers, each a reverent addition. But it was as pointless as if one had tried to arrange grains of sand on the beach; the total effect was colourful, touching but formless. Later additions to the temple looked as if they were imitating a branch of the Midland Bank – a strange reversal of the usual situation, with the Midland trying to be Petra.

Below Kandy we visited the botanical gardens, on the bend of a great muddy river. It was mainly trees and shrubs, some orchids and spices. Well cared for and carefully chosen, it somehow lacked drama; perhaps as Kew has its hothouses, it needed the equivalent of a English garden or something equally bizarre, like those swans at the zoo. But how often again, if it wasn't for a passing palm or coconut, one might not be in England. Maybe it's the rain.

We had lots of rain on the way down to Colombo, and all the rivers suddenly seemed to be in flood; it was alarming when they started slowly eddying across the road too. But by the time we were out of the hills, it was quite dry. It was selective rain again, although at night it was raining hard in the Samudra. The soldiers were still here, and the clerk, but in spite of the advertisements we saw in two newspapers that 'business is as usual', and we were almost the only guests, nothing was functioning at all. Unless this was usual, which seemed unfair. We heard another tale in the hills, that the Samudra belongs to a prominent politician of the opposition, a doctor by profession, and it was rumoured that his practice was going to be annexed, but they had settled for the hotel instead.

On Monday we drove to the High Commissioner's palace on Galle Road, with a trendy 'Dieu et Mon Droit' set into the upper half of an already peeling sixties-style modern shoebox. His representative was affable to the point of actually being helpful and introduced me to a young Sri Lankan archaeologist on the phone. I spent some while talking also to the Defence attaché, who was interested in Chinese porcelain, and who had lots of information about the Maldives and advice on how we should comport ourselves. I felt embarrassed by the length of his discourse, but we still didn't get permission to go to Gan, which was an old outpost in the south; it was still out of bounds. We went back to the Nanking for lunch, but first we made a circuit of the broken walls beneath the bastion of the old Colombo fort; we found several pieces of seventeenth-century blue-and-white in the shitty sand. Peggy found a large section of an eighteenth-century bowl with a wide rim. Then after lunch I went to see the Maldivian Ambassador, who was short and quiet. I tried to tell him what we wanted to do, and he seemed very receptive. But he was worried about where we should live, and suggested we should meet the Chief of Protocol, who was staying with him on a visit from the Maldives.

Then we went to the Archaeological Commission to meet Roland Silva, the Assistant Commissioner. The Commission was in a series of huts on the other side of the road from the National Museum, a rather grand building set in landscaped grounds. I was to get to know it well over the years. Essentially underfinanced and definitely understaffed, it is a miracle that it functioned as well as it did, and almost depended on the Commissioner having independent means. Roland studied architecture at the RIBA, and archaeology at the Institute in London when it was still in its early Regent's Park phase and you could hear the lions roaring in the zoo nearby. He laughs nervously a lot, and tells us he is writing a history of Ceylonese architecture. But we could not find the carved inscriptions from Mantai, or a white Chinese vase mentioned by H. C. P. Bell, an earlier and distinguished colonial Commissioner. He did tell me a lot about the Mannar straits and their importance – apparently this was the main route between India and Sri Lanka until the twelfth century, when the ships engaging in international maritime trade got too large, and had to sail south of Sri Lanka instead. He said there was also another site, south of Mannar, besides Mantai. The Dutch built the fort at Mannar so they could control the passage of shipping. We went to tea with him and met his wife, an opera singer, and his three unruly, cheeky but charming boys. He showed us the measured drawings for his book, made up of plates on average 3 inches by 5 inches, kept in the largest portfolio I have ever seen, leaning against the wall at the foot of their bed. We then had dinner in the Nanking, too, and went to the movies. This was in a nice thirties-style cinema downtown, rather like the one in Alexandria. We saw an American picture about a straight youth who kills a dear old lady in a traffic accident and could do no right ever again. Deservedly.

Early next morning I went to meet the Head of Protocol at the Maldivian Embassy as arranged, but he was not available, and the Ambassador could only spare ten minutes before another appointment. He was very friendly, but still dubious about us finding accommodation on Male. As we left, I smashed the large blue-and-white fragment Peggy had found at the fort, which I had brought to show him, into many more pieces on his door. Then we went to the public library, and read all I could find out about H. C. P. Bell and his work in the Maldives. Bell was the most remarkable man, a Scot, not entirely easy within the official colonial system, but who laid the whole foundations for scientific archaeology in Ceylon. He was indefatigable, dug all the major sites, and had a remarkable record of publishing his discoveries. It was not until he was over seventy that he made his archaeological investigations in the Maldives, in 1922. And when his final work on the Maldives was published in 1940, it was three years after his death.

Most interesting for me was his account of various Buddhist remains he had found throughout the islands, and particularly a 'fine piece of old-time pottery, in white porcelain, cemented into a wall on Gan, in the Hammumati Atoll'. He photographed and measured it and presented it to the National Museum in Colombo in 1922. Fired by this account, after a fish lunch I rushed off to the museum to look for it. But neither the Director nor his assistant could locate it, and it didn't appear in the 1922 list of acquisitions, although the 1923 catalogue contains many Maldivian items given by Bell when he left Ceylon on his retirement. These were mostly ethnographic, but no white porcelain. I did find, however, in the reserves, a group of early celadons, straight-sided carved bowls, and other interesting bits of Chinese material. They were all numbered, but this time we couldn't find the catalogue that related to these particular numbers! The capacity for objects in the National Museum to lose their identity, or to lose themselves completely, was truly incredible. One had the feeling it might not have been so in Bell's time, but who knows?

There was another side to Bell which came out a few years later. He was happily married, and had two daughters who never married and settled in England. Rather late in life they decided they would write the story of their illustrious father, and presented the finished manuscript to the Sri Lankan authorities on the occasion of the hundredth anniversary of the National Museum. There was a party at the British High Commission, which I attended, and there was also an unexpected revelation. It appeared that Bell was not only married but had a number of unofficial native wives, whom he would visit when on circuit to his various archaeological projects round the island, which took up much of his time. In this way there was a whole parallel family of little Bells, first cousins of the two sisters, whom they had never met. It is to their credit that they immediately adopted each other, and thus the two branches were happily reunited at the Commissioner's party.

We had booked a flight to the Maldives for the next day, and at this point we had to abandon Speedy for a while, for there was no future for a motor in the Maldives. We put him to rest in Drummond's Garage in Colombo to await our uncertain return. We had our final dinner in the Samudra, after furtively trying to engage in a bit of black-marketry with some spare dollars we had. But this involved too much dirty work in the dark on the seashore by the Galle Face hotel, and we found the actual rate was not much different to that offered by the shady deal. So we went to bed innocent, to wake up at 3.45am to catch the early morning plane to Male.

6

MALE AND THE MALDIVES

WE WOKE EARLY and waited for the taxi to come at 4.30am, which it did. It had been a very rough night and I could hardly imagine what the flight would be like. We waited at the airport with five Germans bound for paradise, some Maldivians and others. The Ambassador appeared unexpectedly, so early in the morning; he was escorting a young man home for school holidays from London. Again, he told us to get in touch with someone who worked in the customs when we arrived.

We had a surprisingly smooth but lengthy flight, two and a half hours instead of the scheduled one and three quarters, and just enough bumps to remind one what it *could* be like flying in a small plane in the monsoon. Coming down through the clouds we had our first glimpse of the atolls, rimmed with turquoise and greenish-brown under the water, with very pale sand and brilliant green vegetation, mostly coconut palms leaning in the wind. The airport was on the little island of Hulule, half a mile away from Male, the capital of the Maldives. We were almost exactly on the Equator. The Maldives run in a more or less straight north–south line for over five hundred miles, consisting of two thousand islands grouped in atolls – atoll is a Maldivian word. To the north are the Laccadives. All the islands are of coral formation and rise only a few feet above the level of the Indian Ocean; indeed it has been suggested that if there is a general global warming they will disappear altogether. The total population is over a hundred thousand, of whom twenty thousand live on Male alone, which is a mere mile long. Many of the islands are deserted, and there has been a general argument about when they were first settled. The Maldivians speak and write their own language, *Dihevi*, which belongs to the Indo-European family and is closely related to Sinhalese. The present script is based on forms derived from Arabic numerals, and like Arabic is written from right to left.

Islands in the vicinity of the Maldives have been noted since classical times, and Ptolemy lists the names of some of them; the islands were also mentioned by the Chinese traveller Fa-Hsien in the fifth century and again in the sixth century by Cosmas Indicopleustes. The first Arab source is Sulayman, writing in AD 851, who lists 1,900 islands called Dibajat and mentions ambergris, cowry shells and coconuts as their produce, and the skill of the Maldivians in shipbuilding, weaving, and the construction of houses. The Maldivians are indeed skilled craftsmen and must be amongst the finest sailors in the world. Their boats, called *dhonis*, are extremely practical and elegant in design, with a high prow resembling superficially an ancient Egyptian boat. They are constructed of coconut wood, carefully dowled together with sewn planks, with a single mast and a long moveable boom, a rudder at the stern and pairs of oars on either side. Fresh water for long voyages is lashed down onto the deck in large earthenware jars. Indeed, the tale is told of the Maldivian who was blown so far off course that he was picked up off the west coast of Australia, and had to be flown home.

The settlement of the Maldives appears to have coincided with the increasing knowledge of the monsoon winds and how they could be utilised for direct sailing across the Indian Ocean. Bell found the remains of Buddhist stupas on some of the islands, but we have little knowledge of the first settlers. Nor is archaeology likely to be any help here, for the water table is only a few feet below the level of the coral sand, which incidentally provides a filter so that fresh water is available from wells on the inhabited islands. The main source of livelihood is fishing; but as fresh vegetables are few and of poor quality, the diet restricted to fish and coconuts is not particularly healthy and malnutrition is rife on these seemingly idyllic isles; so is Maldivian fever, leprosy and filariasis. Much of this is changing with the introduction of mass tourism on a number of specially designated islands and the efforts of the World Health Organization and other international bodies. This is not to suggest that everyday life is primitive; far from it, for the Maldivians put the limited materials at their disposal to produce highly sophisticated crafts, including textiles, lacquer work, stone and wood carving, and embroidery. A major product, noted at least as early as the ninth century by Sulayman, is the cowry shell. These are the little golden variety *cypraea moneta*, or money cowries, which are collected from the coral outcrops and were used in their tens of thousands as small change in the Indian subcontinent and throughout Asia, as far afield as China and Africa. Ibn Battuta describes their collection and distribution in detail and when he was there in the 1340s the going rate was 1,150 for a gold dinar. He also found the limited diet of fish and coconuts had an agreeable effect on his virility, marrying four times and taking on board a number of concubines as well. One product conspicuously notable for its absence was pottery, for you cannot fashion pots out of coral sand. Although the Maldivians managed to make an ingenious range of vessels and containers from carved wood and even coral stone, pottery really was at a premium, and as we were to discover, a clear indicator of the far-ranging contacts the Maldivians had, not only with India but also the Near and Far East.

All this we were to learn later, but our arrival on Hulule was not encouraging. We tried to explain to the authorities at the airport that we had *no* address and we were *not* going to Bandol, the tourist resort. Eventually someone rang up the contact in the customs, and after a long wait he arrived with his brother-in-law on a fast launch from Male. He was half-bearded, young and rather fierce, and his brother-in-law very young indeed, though he spoke good English which he himself didn't. I tried to explain what we were up to, and showed them a letter I had had some months ago in Maldivian from the Government, saying that they could find us accommodation. The two of them had some quiet conversation, quite short, and to my surprise they said yes, they could find us a place to stay.

We loaded up on to the launch and bounced across the choppy sea to Male; if anything the atmosphere was one of embarrassment. What of course we didn't know was that foreigners were very rare on Male, and normally confined to their tourist traps on other atolls. Nor was there anywhere conventional to stay, like a hotel. When we landed at the little jetty, we set off with the young brother-in-law; he turned out to be seventeen, and was called Mohammed Didi. The significance of being a Didi was that this was the one aristocratic family on the island, even to the extent of speaking in a special Didi-ish manner, rather like Sloane Rangers. In the narrow lanes, all the houses were dazzling, with white walls and new paint; it is Independence Day Thirteenth Anniversary in two days' time, we learned. The walls are all of coral rag oozing slabs of ice-cream between the stones, which on closer inspection revealed itself to be very hard, sharp-edged coral concrete.

Through the open gates of the houses you could see what looked like tilted beds loosely strung with coconut rope; they were open-air sofas. Every garden was so carefully swept and arranged that it was like what I imagined Japanese temples must be. We arrived at a rather grand two-storey house, and it turned out to be Mohammed Didi's. It is one of the few two-storey houses on Male, which he inherited from his father, who was important politically, and also sporting; a pair of carved tennis rackets decorated the pediment. And here was Mohammed's wife, Anisa, who was only sixteen; and here we were to stay. The rest of the morning was spent deciding which rooms we wanted, and what we wanted in them in the way of furniture. We chose one up and one down, each with a bathroom. And we had our own kitchen in an outhouse across the garden. They served us lunch, an assortment of vegetable curries and rice.

Life with the Didis was quite something. They had a car, and a servant (aged twelve) who also doubled up as cook and chauffeur. They were also quite literally bored to tears. Mohammed had no visible occupation or responsibilities, so the whole day was devoted to playing board games, Snakes and Ladders, etc., or playing the gramophone. The Beatles were in vogue that year and they had the lot, and indeed all the young men in Male wore flared *pied d'elephant* trousers with dazzling white shirts in reverence of their idols. The real treat was a bi-annual trip to Colombo, when they could catch up on the latest rock developments. Nor did Mohammed ever fail to let one know that he was a cut above us; but it all broke down when Kathy and Andy were invited to join in the fun and games. The great treat was in the evening, when Mohammed, Anisa, Kathy and Andy would pile into the motor, to be driven by the twelve-year-old a mile or so to the end of the island where there was an ice-cream parlour.

After we had settled in, I went off to explore, and a short walk away found the post office and the tourist agency, the bank, and several shops. These were mostly down on the water's edge, along a street appropriately named Marine Drive. Here also were the Government ministries, all side by side in a new building and labelled 'Health', 'Education', 'Agriculture', etc. This proximity must cut down the inter-ministerial red tape quite a bit. Everything in Male is signposted in Maldivian and English, and all the houses have names. The Maldivian script is often carefully shaded, and looks like jumping jelly-babies. It is all a bit like Toy Town, an atmosphere reinforced by living with the Didis. Outside of a Greek island, I don't think I have ever been anywhere so kempt. The President's Palace is a charming sort of Swiss chalet, gaily painted and beflagged. The Maldivians have an excellent sense of colour, and everything is blue, turquoise or green set off against the white coral, in fact a reflection of the environment itself. Beside the Palace is the tomb of Abu al-Barakat Yusif al-Berberi, who is credited with the conversion of the Maldivians to Islam in the twelfth century. It has splendid new blue doors with silver bosses and lots of white tasselled flags. Opposite is the main mosque, the Friday Mosque, a low, squarish building with a tiered wooden roof now covered with corrugated iron. The general effect is rather like a Buddhist temple. Outside is a cemetery full of blackened coral-stone tombs, covered with lichen. Some are rounded at the top and some pointed, and all carved with the most intricate leafy interlace, quite Celtic in feeling, and inscribed in *Dihevi*. All around the sand has been most carefully swept, with raised stone runways from the ablution well to the doorway of the mosque. Inside were carved wooden posts and beams, all rather low.

There were thirty-three mosques on this tiny island, including five listed by Bell which I could not locate, and again according to Bell some dating as early as the twelfth century and the period of conversion to Islam. When I returned from the Maldives some years later when I was living in Chicago, I received a newspaper cutting from a friend. This was from *Moonlight*, the charmingly named daily paper published in Male, and contained an advertisement for one of the mosques to be put up for auction. I recognised it as a fine fifteenth-century example, and by curious coincidence I had had the same day in the post another letter from the Director of the Kuwait Development Fund. This second friend had been instrumental in the financing of a new international airport in the Maldives, to replace the primitive strip at

Hulule, and knew the islands well. I immediately wrote to him and asked if he could help save the mosque. In the event he was too late, it was auctioned off and dismantled, to be re-erected on a tourist isle as an attraction; however, he did manage to repurchase it, and it was then remantled and taken back to its original home. The point about all this was that the population of Male was steadily growing, and building land in short supply; this also led to many of the cemeteries adjacent to the mosques being cleared, which we were later to find was greatly to our advantage in searching for traces of foreign imports.

Best of all, on the very first day I discovered that the streets of Male are paved with porcelain, or almost. Everywhere in the coral sand little sherds gleam at you, particularly after the daily afternoon shower. You can pick them out of the sandy streets with a sharp point, and from then onwards we were a familiar sight, trailing round the alleys with our shopping bags and kitchen knives. This caused a great deal of mirth amongst the natives, who would stand and giggle at their garden gates. It reduced Andy close to tears, for not only would the boys tease him but also pull his straight blond locks; we solved this problem by buying him a water-pistol to defend himself, which he much enjoyed. As for ourselves, this was surface surveying rather than serious archaeology, but the evidence was there all right, and in quantity.

Back at home, all had been arranged. We began to unpack, and bought a few essential groceries; the shops have limited but expensive supplies of tinned goods, and Danish eggs in sawdust-filled wooden crates. We had bread and cheese for supper in our little hut, and Peggy and I went to bed upstairs in a sort of double cot, but surprisingly comfortable. Lots of the furniture in the house is rather grand, for it now turns out that Mohammed's father was Minister of Finance to the last Sultan (d. 1970) and bought it all in Bombay. He died five years ago, and Mohammed as his only son also inherited five shops; but there is nothing much for him to do, or indeed anywhere to go.

The next day Kathy and Andy woke up covered with bites. After breakfast we went for a walk round the perimeter of the island; there is a new road almost all the way. We picked up more sherds, and after about half a mile we met some workmen and Peggy made our first big find. This was the whole centre of a large celadon plate, being used by the workmen as a cover for their water-pot. To lots of laughter, I bought it by pressing two rupees firmly into the nearest hand. It was actually a fragment of a quite rare *Japanese* celadon dish, probably fifteenth century. Off we went again, and by the time we had circled the island, we had almost forty sherds, all mostly eighteenth century or later, except for the celadon. We shopped for fruit and fish and bought three mackerel-like fish threaded on a loop of string through their noses. We cooked them in our kitchen hut, which we had decided to use as a dining room too. It had a large sink and a triple burner kerosene stove, a long wooden rack for dishes, a table, four chairs and very grubby walls.

We decided we must have sheets, so we shopped for coloured cottons and other things we would need. I bought an eighteenth-century coffee cup full of a dark substance from a betel seller, again for two rupees. I must establish this as the going rate for anything; it's about seven pence. Returning to the house, I spent the rest of the afternoon scrubbing the walls and floor downstairs, to combat the insects and mosquitos. Peggy sewed us all neat pairs of sheets and we were now in very good order.

In the evening, after dinner, Mohammed and Anisa took us off 'shopping'. Although it was 8.30pm all the shops were open, and besides seeing lots we had seen before, we did see the houses of various politicians, all of which were described and itemised for us. Mohammed bought us a beautifully constructed model *dhoni* of plain, unvarnished wood, and about a hundred packets of spearmint chewing gum for Andy, and glasses of sweet orange-coloured pineapple juice for all of us in the only passable cafe. He was very conscious of being of the upper class, and that some things just could not be done. For instance, one is swimming on Male. Another, as Anisa told Peggy, is for a woman to shop; this is for the servants to do. Mohammed also told me about the tourist islands, of which there are now lots. Maldivians can visit them, but as you have to pay for everything in foreign currency, this is a limitation. We turned back from our guided tour just as the President and his entourage arrived back cheerfully on a fast launch from one of these islands, Bandol.

Next day was Independence Day, everything looking very gay and everybody smartly dressed, I walked out to the Sultana's tomb, or what was left of it, near the radio station. It consisted of three parts, small concrete enclosures about two feet high on the edge of a sports ground by the radio aerials. The headstones had been recently smashed; I had asked Mohammed about this the previous night when we had passed them in the dark and he had unconvincingly replied 'lightning'. Today the tombs were full of real lightning in force – kids. They were using the enclosures as Maldivian play centres. I pieced the headstones together by balancing the fragments on top of one another, looking sternly at the children and wagging my finger. It wouldn't do much good beyond giving them a momentary bad conscience. It began to rain very hard, and I took shelter in a timber yard. It was deserted except for a soldier on duty at the gate. It was now raining so heavily that I settled under a thatched hut and discovered the most beautiful big boat being hewn out under it. As far as I could see, the *dhoni* was made entirely by accurate jointing and dowelling of the wood, each piece chopped and sawn to fit. It really was a piece of sculpture, and the curving lines infinitely subtle though produced by the crudest hatchet work. The rain stopped, but as I continued it came on again and I arrived back dripping.

After lunch we went on another long drizzly walk, and had our first success in a garden being dug to plant trees. Then we found more sherds in an adjacent mosque, which turned out to be typical of most mosques on the island; all the tombstones in the cemeteries outside were being cleared, the soil dug down a foot or so and then replaced with fine coral gravel. Where the tidying up hadn't been completed there were masses of sherds, including some celadon. We moved entranced from mosque to mosque, and our shopping bag got heavier and heavier. They were also more interesting and earlier as we moved towards the old Palace, now dismantled, and the grounds turned into the Sultan's park, a garden aglow with flowers and little walkways. It began to rain and we got back home just in time. I decided to tackle the mosque next to our house, which I could see from our bedroom window, as a final fling. And what appeared from the cemetery, from a pile of rubble and broken headstones, but two sherds, of a bowl and a plate, of the finest early Yuan celadon! One piece was stamped with a lotus design inside and carved outside with radiating petals, the other with a faint but elegant classic scroll design on the rim. Suddenly it became clear what we must do – we must dig a few well-placed holes. Already we must have collected over two hundred sherds.

After Indepedence Day was over everything was shut except for a few shops. We wandered around the market and found a smoked fish speared lengthwise on palm slivers, scored neatly across and filled with a red peppery paste. It was quite good re-heated but must have been much better hot. I scoured a building site or two with not great success, finding only small late pieces. After lunch we went for a long expedition to the other end of the island. Here land was being reclaimed from the sea by building out coral walls on to the reef and filling in with tip, cemetery tip some of it, for it contained pottery and a piece of a gravestone. Visiting the cemeteries round the mosques it was clear what was happening. Land was so scarce that the cemeteries were being contracted, the land dug and cleared to a depth of half a metre or so, and then sold off. Some mosques hadn't yet had this done; others already had new buildings going up on the old land. We had arrived just at the right moment.

As we walked down the main longitudinal street across the island we saw a hospital ambulance with a coffin and mourners; and when we arrived at the cemetery near the reclaimed land, they had already started the burial service. As the cemetery seemed unusually high, we waited until the service was over and then went inside. This new cemetery consisted of about a metre of soil taken from the old cemeteries, inside a high wall; and the soil was studded with pottery. Feeling rather ghoulish, we went around with our shopping bags, picking up all the sherds we could see.

We walked back along the coast and past the boats in the harbour just as the fishing fleet was coming in. Hundreds of silvery fish, tuna perhaps, were being carted to the market place, and we bought a small one for a rupee. On the way home we heard the sound of drums and a procession, and we walked to the end of our street to see what was up. Everyone was out dressed in their very best, and first the boys' school and then the girls' school paraded, looking very smart and marching very straight, with their two bands. The girls even had a baton-twirler; the boys, a Sri Lankan officer with a very sharp, drawn silver sword. We wanted to go to the cinema in the evening, but the programme had been cancelled for a loyal manifestation instead. We met a Sri Lankan teacher and his wife in the crowd; he taught in a private English school, and they turned out to be renting another house, belonging to Mohammed's aunt. She spoke some Maldivian, he a little, and both said it wasn't difficult if you knew Sinhalese. We found a grocer round the corner who spoke English and made shirts when business was slack. We bought a palm basket from him and a wooden spoon made out of half a coconut shell pierced with a stick.

The sun shone again after yesterday's rain, and I made a list of all the people we should see. First I went to the WHO office, to meet the English doctor; he said a year and a half in the Maldives seems longer than the seventeen years he previously spent in Malaysia. He lived in a string of rented cottages on the other side of the island diametrically across the road from his office, near the reclaimed land. He seemed vague and nervous, but full of interesting snippets of information. He told me that the nearest place I wanted to go, on South Male, was full of leprosy.

Next I went on to the ministries, all of which I had already noted were in a two-storey building near the sea and all conveniently next door to each other, so it was rather like knocking doors in a suburban street. On the ground floor of each one were the minor underlings and the secretaries, and upstairs the Secretary/Minister/Director. I started with the man who signed the letter I received last February, but he had been promoted to Planning, and was not available. I went on to Information, who promised maps and permission to dig in the Sultan's Garden, tomorrow. Then I proceeded to Finance, to see the Minister, who was also in charge of Religious Affairs; but he was not there, come back later. Then to External Affairs, where I met a lady secretary who was both helpful and intelligent. Back to Finance where I was sent off to another building; here the responsible Minister gave us permission to sift through all the rubbish in the mosque courtyards. What is more, he promised to let us have someone to go with us, and also to send a message to all the mosques (there are quite a few) telling them to look for porcelain on our behalf. He also reiterated the suggestion made by External Affairs, that we get Radio Maldives to broadcast an appeal for Chinese pots! And also to put an advertisement in *Moonlight*, the daily newspaper.

After lunch, I met the Minister's representative, a young clerk, who had arrived by bicycle at the gate of the Hadibi mosque opposite our back door. Besides explaining what we were up to to the curious congregation, he insisted on helping himself when I started to dismantle the tidy pile of gravestones, bones and pottery in the corner of the cemetery. Andy organised the local children as well and in no time we had an unpaid chain gang hard at work. There was a pause whilst evening prayers took place, then we worked on until five, having half finished sifting through the whole large pile. When we washed and sorted the results back home, it really was an interesting group of material. There was everything from fourteenth-century celadon, a piece of Annamese ware, and the fifteenth through to the eighteenth centuries all well represented. I also dug a small hole in the cemetery, but after half a metre or so found it still quite sterile sand, so everything we found must have come from the topsoil and the graves which had been removed. After we had finished for the day, we went at six to the WHO doctor for a drink. He had more tales to tell, and I would have liked to have stayed longer, but he seemed rather reserved and not the sort of person one could linger with at first acquaintance. He was going on leave in a couple of weeks anyhow, so he wouldn't be much use for inter-island transportation. I had almost enough sherds already from Male to tell the tale, but it would be nice to have some pre-fourteenth-century material and some early blue-and-white. Perhaps the Palace site in the Sultan's Garden will be the answer.

I went back the following day to the Ministry of Information, but now they wanted an official letter of application to dig in the Sultan's Garden, which I dutifully composed; judgement would be passed tomorrow. A labourer cost only four rupees a day, so excavation would be no great expense; nor effort, as the sandy soil was only a metre deep and very loose. Dr WHO said that the Japanese effect I had noticed in the gardens of private houses was simply because the garden is used as an outside toilet, and gets swept over freshly each time. The assistant clerk in the Ministry produced more books about the Maldives and reports by Bell, and I traced the map of the town from his book, as well as the Palace section of a modern map the clerk had, which unfortunately had no scale. I also made sketches of Bell's two photographs of the Palace from outside the walls, when it was still standing. From the north there appeared to be an outer and smaller high-walled inner enclosure, with a two-storeyed building and sort of pavilion in front of it. From the south-west angle, there was a large tree (which must still be there) and a larger building with a pitched roof south of the other two buildings, perhaps the kitchen quarters? Mohammed Zahir, the assistant, said that the kitchens were supposed to have been near the new tennis courts, which are on the west side. I went for a walk in the garden and picked up some blue-and-white, mostly late. On the west side near the tennis courts there were a couple of bits of celadon, one with a foliate rim, so maybe this would be a good place to start. I measured the length of the present west wall of the garden, and back in the house tried to reduce the modern map to the same scale as the one in Bell's publication. This was not easy, as the two did not correlate at all well. I finally concluded that the Palace area had been enlarged on the east and west sides to make the present garden, and re-aligned on the south side. The only safe thing to do for a start would be a line of trenches east–west across the middle of the overlapping sites; this would be feasible, as there was a modern path there and it wouldn't mean wrecking the garden. The garden was in full flower, and very pretty and peaceful; nobody seemed to use it at all during the three hours it was officially open in the late afternoon. It was full of little walks and pools, and quite delightful in a toy-like way; it would be an exceedingly pleasant place to dig, amongst the flowers.

After lunch we returned to the mosque next door, to finish sorting the cemetery debris. We had a rather obnoxious commentary from waves of schoolchildren, more daring now that Mohammed Zahir wasn't with us. Towards the end I had to move increasingly heavy tombstones, no joke with a giggly audience. But the same flock of faithful men came to evening prayers and they were very friendly. Whilst they prayed, we stopped for tea. When we had finally cleared the corner, I set to, to dig a hole down to the original coral sand. I was only 70cm down when the grey sand and soil turned to pure white coral sand, but it was all mixed up with brown human bones, so I hastily filled it in again. This must have been the general burial level judging by the burial the other day, when they finished off the mound by powdering it with fresh white sand, so one should not deduce that I had got down to the natural sand level in the cemetery. For all this digging, the only interesting finds were a couple of sherds of celadon, a delicately moulded base sherd and part of the foliate rim of a dish. But as a whole the group from the Hadibi mosque is an impressive survey from the fourteenth century onwards, worth publishing by itself as a corpus to show the diversity of the material from a single location.

Whether or not from exhaustion or emotion, I had an alarming experience in the night. I felt I was slipping, sinking away, and getting cold from the feet upwards. I woke Peggy and she was equally disturbed by this strange experience and we passed a fitful night. I was glad to see the day.

I went back to the Ministry of Information, to find my request had been passed on to the Prime Minister, and he had replied that the garden was dug four or five feet deep and all the 'vases and plates' that were found sold at auction in Male; indeed, auction sales for incredible rubbish take place frequently on the edge of the firewood bazaar. I countered by sending him word that even little pieces were enough for me, and *please* could I dig between the tennis courts? I found out from Bell that until the late nineteenth century the Palace was surrounded by a moat on three sides, which then filled up with weeds and was finally filled in. As the garden appeared to be larger to east and west than the Palace area, a trench on the west side would theoretically traverse the moat, hit the foundations of the wall, and continue inside the Palace grounds at the point where the kitchens were reputed to have been. I spent the rest of the morning reading Bell's account of his visit in 1921, his first since his previous one in 1896. It is an excellent record, and he gives details of all the mosques as they were then. There were thirty-three of them.

With notes of his account in hand and a copy of his map, we set off in the afternoon to work systematically through his list, and check at what stage of clearance each mosque had got.

We did most of them on the west side of the island, and found one which was being heavily built over, with quantities of pottery on the surface. I found a base sherd of celadon of very fine quality moulded with a floral design. On our wanderings, we met Dr WHO again on his bicycle, who invited us to supper the next day to meet an English teacher and his Maldivian wife, and an English lady doctor who was a leprosy specialist. We met him yet again when we were looking for a water tank, now completely disappeared, and went to have an orangeade with him. Previously, another man on a bicycle had lured us half a mile away to a tiny thatched cottage with a promise of a pot 'two hundred years old'. We sat expectantly in his yard, on one of the coconut-fibre outdoor sofas, surprisingly comfortable. He produced a crackled, glazed pot with a thick rim, showing every sign of age; a noble, simple form. It was an English pudding bowl, with BRITISH MADE stamped on the base. I did spy a baby sucking away at a coffee cup, brown on the outside and blue within, like the one I had bought from the betel man. But then they produced another similar one and I began to have doubts; perhaps they were modern imitations of eighteenth-century ones. Feeling confused we retired to the market. Peggy bought a Maldivian dress for $10, with a deep, stiff collar of silver embroidery. The same man also had some pretty, simple lacquer boxes, and two pairs of flippers, no doubt left over by passing tourists. He also had lots of little coins in a box, with Arabic inscriptions which I took to be Maldivian. We bought our first potatoes, two pounds for three rupees, and three fish for half a rupee for supper. I felt very tired and went to bed, and a fever soon came on.

All next day in bed the fever continued unabated, curiously reluctant to respond to repeated dosage of Aspirins. It came down slightly in the evening, but I didn't feel well enough to go out to dinner. Most of the day I half-slept and had gloomy thoughts, which seemed to go with my condition. It was a horrid day anyhow, grey and humid with occasional showers. Peggy had a rich dinner and when she came home promptly

Plate 1 Chinese porcelain dish from Damascus

FRANÇOIS OFFICE
for
Car driving Lessons

Hamra Street – Capucin Bldg.

Tel. 256683

BEIRUT – LEBANON

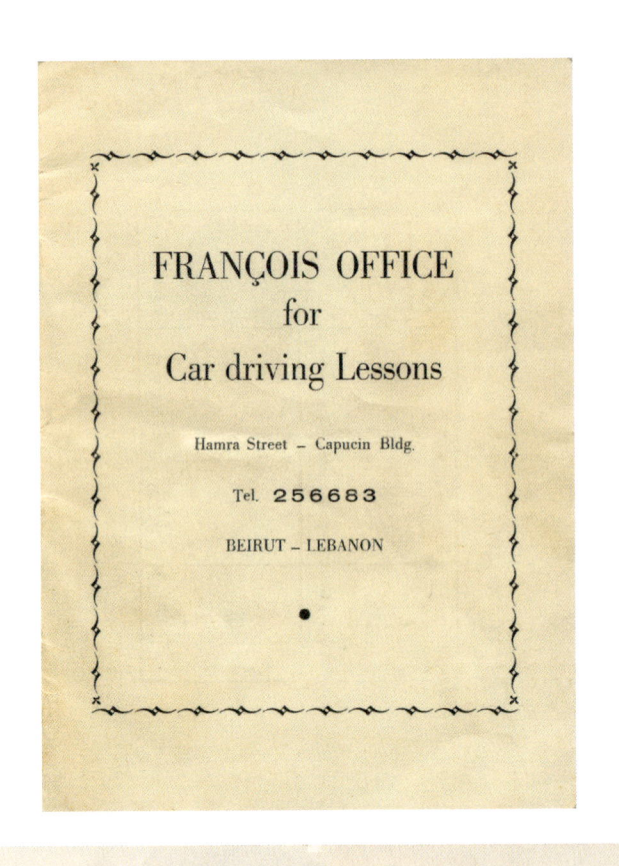

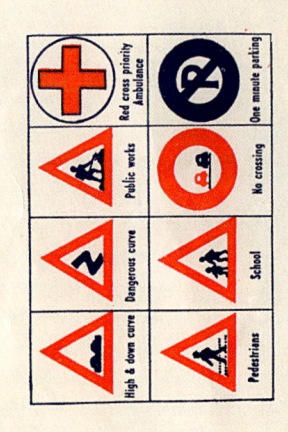

ROAD REGULATIONS

Q. – How many public roads are there in town?
A. – All town roads are public.
Q. – If two meet on a cross road who should pass first?
A. – The one whose right is clear.
Q. – What is meant by "his right is clear"?
A. – That is the cross road on his right should be empty of cars.
Q. – To which direction he can go?
A. – To any direction he wishes.
Q. – If four meet on four cross roads, who should pass first?
A. – The four should stop and agree which one should pass before, and then the one whose right becomes free follows.
Q. – Do you have the right of passing on the right side of the tram?
A. – I can pass on the right and left side of the tram if it is running.
Q. – Which is preferable passing on the right or left?
A. – On the left, since the left side of the tram is wider and the tram is closed which prevents the going up and down of the passengers.
Q. – How do you pass on the right side of the tram?

– 1 –

Plate 2 M. Francois' driving instructions

Plate 3 Peggy and the Morgan in Beirut, across from the Intercontinental Hotel (left) and a nightclub (right)

Plate 4 John at Tabarja, across the bay from our house on the left

Plate 5 Inside our house at Tabarja, looking into our bedroom, the balcony and the bay on the left

Plate 6 The Waif: Andy with his broken arm in a sling

Plate 7 On the road: Speedy in the foreground, in the Taurus Mountains, Turkey

Plate 8 A close-up of Speedy, with Martha and Peggy, and Andy sitting on the bumper

Plate 9 Andy's interpretation of Speedy, driving at night

Plate 10 The Suq al-Hamidiyeh in Damascus. It was off an alley on the right that I found my first broken fourteenth-century Chinese blue-and-white dish

Plate 11 The fourteenth-century Chinese blue-and-white dish which nearly crashed onto the marble floor in Henri Pharaon's house in Beirut. It is now in the Art Institute of Chicago

Plate 12 In Kuwait, driving across the sand to SS Dwarka

Plate 13 Loading Speedy aboard, minus luggage and passengers

Plate 14 In the jungle in south India, Andy discovered a group of extraordinary terracotta horses

Plate 15 In Male in the Maldives, the Hadibi mosque, looking down from our room in the Didi house. Note the scoops, of half coconut shells attached to long poles, on top of the well

Plate 16 Andy and a gang of Maldivian boys at the well

Plate 17 Mohamed Didi's gift of a model dhoni, *complete with a moveable rudder, an anchor, oars and miniature fishing tackle*

Plate 18 The real thing: a group of dhonis *and fishermen in the harbour in Male*

Plate 19 The celadon base sherd used as a stopper for a water jar

Plate 20 The white porcelain stem cup

Plate 21 A Maldivian lacquer box and cover containing cowry shells (cipraea moneta)

Plate 22 Maldivian carved coral gravestones in the cemetery adjacent to a mosque

Plate 23 A set of eight Persian Safavid seventeenth-century dishes and one later Chinese Swatow dish, purchased in Male by the author

Plate 24 A Maldivian Chess board purchased in Male by the author. Carved out a hard wood, probably teak, with designs resembling those on Maldivian gravestones; the red and yellow pieces are of typical local enamelled ware

Plate 25 The crash – the end of Speedy, with an amused spectator having his photo taken

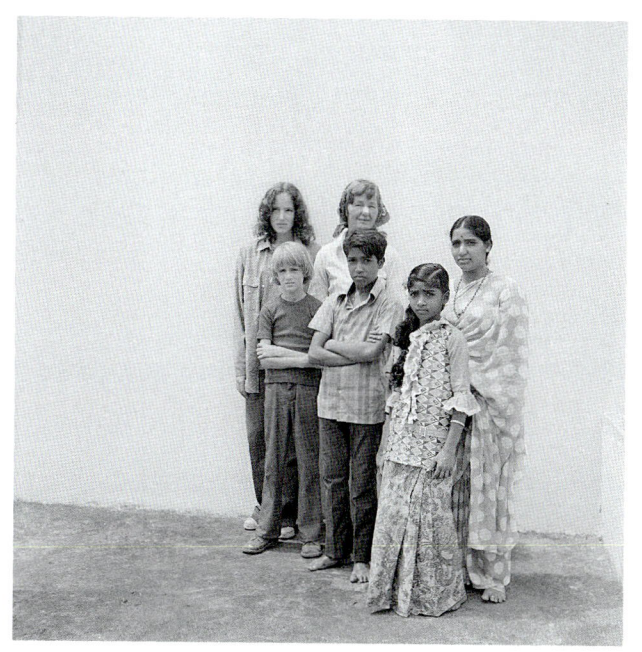

Plate 26 We were befriended by a local family near Tarikere. Martha and Andy are on the left

Plate 27 Street scene in Beirut during the civil war

Plate 28 The envelope containing the invitation to the opening of the new Islamic Gallery at the Metropolitan Museum in New York. The Hezbollah had removed the stamps ...

retired to the bathroom and was sick. It would take us months of reconditioning to learn how to eat again! She met the English teacher married to the Maldivian, and the English public health nurse leaving next year to be a student at LSE. The Maldivian teacher wanted me to talk to her class, which was in the school beside the Sultan's Garden.

Again the following day I was still sick. According to my intake of Veganin, my temperature varied between 100–102°. I read a lot of Tolkein to decide most of it is a bore, at least in my mood. He also has a prickly introduction which puts one off a bit. I found an Agatha Christie which was more relaxing and better written anyhow. I wrote to Charles Wilkinson and Irma, and Gerald Harding. Sick after lunch, Peggy and the children went to Hulule to see what the swimming was like, and I fell asleep. It was dark when they returned. During the day a note had arrived in reply to the one I had sent to the Ministry of Information, explaining why I hadn't called on them about the proposed excavation:

MINISTRY OF INFORMATION
MALE.
August 1st, 1974.

Dear Mr. John Carswell,

I am very sorry to hear that you are not been fit. But I hope with the help of God Almighty you would soon be better.

With regard to the little excavation you intended to make in Sultan's Garden, I wish to inform you that the Under Secretary would like to know the exact permission before he could grant permission.

Hence, please let me know when you could come and see me to go and locate the place.

Yours sincerely,
MOHAMED ZAHIR
Secretary.

I found the style of his letter very impressive, as he had told me he was entirely educated in the local school. I also found that the hundred or so paperbacks and thrillers in the house we are staying in are all Mohammed Didi's own, which is not bad for 17.

The fever lasted several days more, and I felt very limp. I wrote to Gerald Reitlinger, telling him the streets are paved with porcelain, which would amuse him, and to Hamid and Eva, his Swedish girlfriend, that we did actually get here; it seemed an awful long way from Beirut, and we have to get back again. The next night I had a very damp, feverish sleep induced by Veganin, and after an early shower I decided the time had come for professional advice. I went to the hospital, where they did a blood count; it was normal. The whole thing was a mystery, as my temperature was a steady 101–102° with no other real symptoms. Peggy was busy stitching away at a tablecloth and napkins for a feast in the future, which at least was cheerful. Kathy and Andy went swimming early in the morning with Mohammed and his wife, to Hulule, and came back at lunch rather burnt.

I started taking antibiotics, with some effect; I felt much better during the day and the temperature at last began to go down. I read and read, and started a plan of the mosque across the road, but it wouldn't come out right with the measurements I had. I made a couple of drawings of the celadon, experimenting with a technique to show the moulded patterns. For the first time I slept without waking, and then next morning, surprise, my temperature was normal. I still felt very weak but progressively steadier during the day. I made it as far as the Ministry of Information, and we walked with Mohamed to the Sultan's Garden and showed him where we intended to dig; he said he would let us know tomorrow. I drew a bit more of the mosque plan, and we visited some more to note the state of their cemeteries. We now had two Sri Lankan school teachers in the outhouse across the back yard; they arrived without cholera shots and were now in quarantine for a week. The back gate was locked and there was a warning notice nailed to the wall telling the public what had happened. It seemed as if the Didi house was the solution to everyone's accommodation problems, ours included. I called at one of the agencies for the tourist islands and discovered that a boat and crew would cost $60 a day! I was now completely recovered, but then Andy announced he has a fever, and neatly took my place.

We went to Radio Maldives and met the young, bearded Director, Mr Mustafa. He had been to school in Sri Lanka and afterwards spent three years in Australia, and he was very friendly and efficient. He arranged for three broadcasts to follow the news for three days running, nine in all, which cost us 14.31 rupees for the lot – just over $2. I gave him the gist of what I wanted to say, to encourage people to show us their pots, and he translated all this into *Dihevi*. He himself came from an island in the atoll north of Bandol. We tried more boat agents during the day and the best quote we could get was $44 for a diesel boat. No one would take us on an ordinary boat to a tourist island; we would have to investigate transport somehow lower down the scale.

I made some more measurements for my mosque plan, and best of all Mohamed Zahir says we can dig. We agree to meet at 1.30pm in the garden. In the meantime, buying coconut string and stakes to mark out the trenches, the shop owner mysteriously produces nine very weathered Persian seventeenth-century dishes. I agreed to return in the afternoon to find out how much he wanted for them. And in the road Peggy found the rim of a celadon bowl with moulded vertical panels, a new type.

After lunch I met Mohamed and a man from the Works Department – apparently the tennis courts came under separate jurisdiction. He turned out to be the brother of a student from the American University in Beirut, Mohamed Hassan Manik, who arrived back home today. The Works Department agreed to the dig, and would also provide workers free, which was a big relief, so we could dig two pits at once. Like our visit to the Radio Station, it all seemed so simple once it got going.

Later we returned to the shop to discuss the Persian plates. The man produced a further collection of Chinese polychrome bowls and plates, eighteenth/nineteenth century, all in very good condition, for $25 to $50 each. These I declined, but bought all the Persian ones from him for $3 for the lot; one was actually Chinese, a little Swatow dish. They presented a problem, for they were the *only* pieces of Islamic pottery we had found so far, and there had been nothing amongst the sherds we had collected. Perhaps these whole pieces were a unique hoard in the Palace; they were very weathered and must have been buried as a cache at some time. Nothing about trade with the Islamic world in general can be deduced from them, but they do demonstrate how far eastwards Persian pottery of the Safavid period had penetrated. They must have been of the second half of the seventeenth century as two of them had landscape designs with washes of cobalt blue which were directly based on Chinese ware of the 'transitional' period. That the Maldivians had direct contact with the Persian Gulf we learned from Bell, who records that 'Abd-ur-Razzak mentions traders from the "islands of Diva-Mahal" (that is, the Maldives) were amongst foreign merchants at the emporium of Hormuz, in 1492'. This, of course, is a couple of hundred years earlier than the plates.

Earlier in the day I had my first caller in response to the broadcasts. He actually worked at Radio Maldives as a technician, and he brought me a modern fragment and a very pretty celadon stem-cup, which he gave me. My first reaction was that it must be early, but this judgement was tempered when I saw it had a white porcelain body, rather than the more typical pale grey of the Yuan and early Ming dynasties.

We were due to start digging the next day at 8.30am. Incidentally, yesterday workmen were digging a hole in the road just about where the little bastion tower outside the

Palace gates used to be. They reached lighter sand and water just over a metre down; otherwise it was all dark sand, with a very dark horizontal layer about 50cm below the surface. Quite a few odd sherds and stones came up. They then proceeded to fill the hole with burial rubbish, I think from Hemvem 16, where the cemetery was being cleared at the moment.

It was very hot today and the sunlight was blinding, reflected from the whitewashed walls; it burns in no time at all. There was no rain until after dark. On the south side of the island this morning the tide was a long way out, and all the women and children were amongst the coral rocks in the shallows panning the sand, it was not clear for what. Ibn Battuta describes women preparing coconut fibre to make coir ropes 'in trenches near the shore', and also gathering cowries from the sea, which they put into pits dug on the shore until the flesh decays and only the shell remains.

I arrived next morning in the garden early, at 8 o'clock, and found I was alone. By 9 o'clock I went to find Mohamed in desperation; he was surprised, and after telephoning around he said that two workers were supposed to be there. So we returned to the garden and waited and eventually two lads turned up; they were actually the boys who looked after the tennis courts. I marked out two trenches, each two metres by one metre, about twenty-five metres apart from each other, theoretically according to my plans one inside and one outside the old Palace wall. The first trench was slow going, with practically no pottery at all; it was in the sun and got very hot by 11.30. A wall appeared at the east end, running across the trench at a slight angle. After lunch, we started on the second trench, as it was in the shade of a very large tree, one of the largest on the island. A little way down, still with no pottery, the tree-roots appeared. The boys good-naturedly hacked away at them, but eventually we abandoned it for the day.

Andy was now sick with my complaint, including the strange hallucinating symptoms. At least we now knew how to cure him. Back to the digging, we finished the first trench, which eventually became waterlogged, as we reached the water table. Below the wall, which was two courses high, and the stones of the upper one bevelled back at the top, there is a level of light sand about 10cm deep, probably a courtyard. And below this the soil was darker and as we got lower filled with pottery. There were also four pieces of off-white glazed ware, three with stoneware bodies and the fourth of yellow earthenware with a white slip. The rest of the pottery consisted of reddish earthenware, rims of cooking pots and jars. The other trench we abandoned completely, and the first one would have to do for our general *sondage*.

Although I later claimed in a lecture to the Oriental Ceramic Society in London that this *sondage* was the smallest excavation east of Suez in 1974, it turned out to be not without interest. What we had discovered in the way of pottery, scanty though it was, belonged to a period earlier than the wall, which was probably part of a building within the Palace enclosure. It was the four whitish sherds which were diagnostic, for later on our trip I was to find surface pottery at a site near Vankalai on the coast of north-west Sri Lanka which tied in exactly with the three white stoneware sherds; the fourth must obviously have been Islamic, but of the same period. As for the red earthenware, this was also similar to the local pottery from that site. I dug the site itself some years later, in 1977, and determined that it was a little settlement which probably lasted only fifty years or so, in the early twelfth century. This then was the date of our material from the lower level of the Sultan's Garden, more or less the period when the Maldivians were converted to Islam. The earthenware was also typical of that manufactured in Sri Lanka, in styles unchanging over the centuries. As the Maldivians had no pottery of their own, the pottery we found was exactly the type that they would have imported from Sri Lanka and even further afield. Again, Ibn Battuta tells how they bought pottery from visiting boats, and that a cooking pot (*kidr*) would be bartered for five or six chickens. Concerning Ibn Battuta and the Maldives, there have been some sceptics who have argued that he never visited the islands and that all his information was gathered at second hand. A similar accusation has more recently been made about Marco Polo's travels to China. But our experience, even though limited, showed so much of what he described in the fourteenth century to be true to what we know of local customs and tradition today that it left me with no doubt that he did actually visit the Maldives and his account of his experiences is an authentic one.

In the afternoon, having finished our little dig, we took a boat to Hulule and walked right down to the southern tip of the airport runway and up the eastern side of the island. There were masses of beautiful shells, and also a simple little village. It was a relief to be away from Male, even if only briefly, and made one long to have the means to visit some of the other atolls and islands. I had decided that I did not like Male; so many people living on dirty coral sand for centuries, being buried in it and drinking water filtered through it. The superficial whitewashing and spick-and-span appearance could not conceal the fact of too many people living too close to each other in too little space. Apart from the few friends we made, the people as a whole were not particularly friendly and even rather aggressive in their comments; the children were downright cheeky and rude. This of course can be partly explained by the fact that we were unfamiliar, just as much a curiosity as a black man was in eighteenth-century England. But the atmosphere is claustrophobic, and just to walk by the sailing boats in the harbour made one long to leave, in any direction. And I thought we would, on Sunday, as we had more than enough evidence to prove my point about the China trade.

I made a final plan and sections of the trenches in the garden. Later, I took many photographs of the port, of *dhonis* with *martaban* jars lashed down to the deck, and fruit and chickens, sea turtles, coconuts and dried fish in the market. Peggy bought a very handsome black and brown striped cloth for $5. Then we went for a final visit to the mosques being cleared, found more celadon and other bits and pieces, including the only fragment which might be a candidate for fourteenth-century Chinese blue-and-white ware. A boy came running up with a plastic bag full of indifferent sherds and a discoloured eighteenth-century bowl, but worth having for the cursive Chinese inscription on the base; it was the same type as a couple of other sherds which had turned up. I made measured drawings of the cooking pots and four white sherds from the garden, and finished the plan and section of the mosque across the road, and measured the levels of the cemetery, cleared and uncleared, and the road outside. It was obvious that the road level was well below the level of the soil in most cemeteries before they were dismantled. The general water level was about 80cm below the surface, but this must vary seasonally, and in the garden it was more like a metre down. That night we went for our last visit to the cinema and saw a fatuous film with Audrey Hepburn.

Next day was our last day and we went to the airport office to buy tickets. We were alarmed to find the plane was fully booked, but the clerk relented and agreed that some passengers were not serious; the three and a half fares came to £65, one-way Male–Colombo. We broke the news to Mohammed Didi that we were leaving, and he charged us 20 rupees a day for our stay, as we didn't stay a whole month and qualify for the reduced rate of 500 rupees, fair enough. There was also a belated 30 rupees to pay for the launch the first day, which apparently was a non-optional extra.

We bought an old Maldivian chess board, the ends carved with leafy motifs like those on the coral tombstones. I took numerous photographs of the mosques, cemeteries, gravestones and general clearance. Little did I know at the time that everything I took with my Rolleiflex came out, but all the 35mm slides when developed turned out to be perfectly exposed half-transparencies; the shutter had been failing throughout the trip. I finished all my plans and notes, and took a compass bearing on the Hadibi mosque. It was hot; down by the sailing boats, each *dhoni* was a little world in itself, like a floating house. I had real regrets we never managed to see the islands in one of them, particularly as I could not see we would ever return to the Maldives. What happens to the Maldives is going to depend on the younger generation; there seemed to be a tremendous gap between the smart young like Mohamed and his wife, and the islanders on their cosy boats with the fisherman's traditional way of life. Tourism will inevitably inject an explosive note.

Next morning we flew off after an interminable wait on Hulule, with two well-built Italian *signorinas* and a lot of tanned French. We bumped along at the wrong altitude and arrived, all of us with headaches, about lunchtime, and celebrated our return with several cups of tea at the airport. We were back at the Samudra, where we were welcome, the strike seemed to have passed over. It seemed like luxury to be back in the seedy surroundings of the converted tea-planters club, after our time in Male.

When I came to write up the results of our expedition some months later, the role of the Maldives in maritime trade between the Near and Far East became clearer. The clue was the *absence* of Islamic pottery (and glass) amongst our street finds. This meant there was a pattern of trade from east to west, but not the other way. Why? The answer was simple and concerns the monsoons. Such is the direction of the winds, if you sail from the Red Sea or Persian Gulf across the Indian Ocean, you can only reach south India or Sri Lanka on one monsoon. There you have to wait out the inter-monsoon period, until the second, reverse monsoon carries you on to the Far East and ultimately China. But the reverse is not true, for if you return by the north-east monsoon and reach the Straits of Malacca by a certain season of the year, you can get to India and the Near East *on one monsoon*. But in order to do so, you have to sail far south of Sri Lanka, in fact right through the middle of the Maldives. These facts were noted by the famous Arab navigator Ahmad Ibn Majid, writing about 1490; Ibn Majid knew what he was talking about, for it was he that guided the Portuguese fleet across the Indian Ocean, which changed the whole balance of power in the late fifteenth century. Moreover, in Tibbett's commentary on Ibn Majid, he notes that you can get from Malacca to Jiddah and up the Red Sea in one voyage, using the technique of *takkiya*, or tacking, to move against the prevailing north wind. The importance of the Maldives, and Male in particular, is further exemplified by an early sixteenth-century Chinese map, which is generally considered to be based on the emperor Cheng Hua's expeditions to the west, conducted by his admiral, Ma Huan. This map shows all the traffic from China passing south of Sri Lanka to Male, where the routes then divided to East Africa, and Quilon and Cape Comorin in south India, and other destinations to the west.

What was the importance of Male? First, here travellers could get fresh water, after a long journey across the ocean from south Asia; this explains the large number of water jars still in use today, of Malaysian origin. Secondly, there was always the possibility of some trade for fresh provisions, bartering Chinese ware perhaps for Maldivian products. And thirdly, as Ibn Battuta points out in his usual forthright way, 'when vessels arrive, the members of the crew take women, and when they leave they repudiate them; it is a kind of temporary marriage. The Maldive women never leave their country'. And finally, as many of the sailors on these long voyages were Muslims, the Maldives possessed a real advantage by being populated by their co-religionists, unlike the alien inhabitants of India and Sri Lanka. For almost two thousand years, the Maldives were bang in the middle of the main route from China to the West.

7

SRI LANKA AGAIN

IN COLOMBO my first visit was to the British Consulate, to get my passport renewed. A middle-aged lady made all sorts of murmurs, so much work, and quite out of the question immediately; I capitulated and agreed to return tomorrow. Then we went off to the garage where we had left the car. We had a joyful reunion with Speedy; Mr Peiras had done a splendid job, for not very much money. The car was perfectly in tune, and the parts they couldn't replace, they had made. Mr Peiras has motors written all over his face, and the whole garage reflected his enthusiasm, the general morale very similar to that at Morgan Motors.

We set off for the museum and the Archaeological Commission. Both Roland Silva, and Raja de Silva, the Commissioner, were away, Raja on circuit. I had particularly wanted to talk to Raja as he had organised the recent dig at Mantai, which had produced the Arabic inscribed slab. I tried to locate the fourteenth-century porcelain that was said to have been excavated at Polonnaruwa, but the best anyone could suggest were three celadon bowls said to be in the museum in Anuradhapura. There were odd snippets of information, of Chinese coins and sherds from other sites, but nothing had been systematically classified, and there was obviously much work to do correlating all the different material. There was even a reference to Mamluk coins being found in Sri Lanka.

At this point, before returning to India we decided to make a rough circuit of the island, setting off south for Galle. First we collected my passport and spent all morning posting packages back to ourselves in Beirut, to reduce the weight in the car. We had a picnic lunch in the bedroom of the Samudra, and reached Ambalagoda in the late afternoon. The shabby rest house was in a spectacular spot, with three sandy coves and the rocks ringed with thousands of drunken coconut palms. There was a fishing village with the most curious catamarans, which had been beached for the windy season and neatly thatched to protect them. We walked through the village to a famous mask maker, and saw the various stages of production. It started with a store of tree trunks (rather like the Morgan Motor Works), then roughly carved masks which were laid over with a coat of plaster. Finally the paint was applied coat by coat, and the finished effect both refined and dramatic. We bought a devilish green one for Andy. Back through the village there were a few odd shops with nothing of great interest, but seeming like goldmines to us after the paucity of the shops in Male. At the rest house we had a 'European' dinner of breaded fish cutlets with a few shrimps for decor. It was appropriately expensive, as we discovered when we came to pay the bill next day.

Leaving all the luggage in the rest house after a hard bed and a hard night, we took Speedy south to the old Dutch town of Galle, which had been surprisingly well preserved since it was established in the seventeenth century. The Dutch fort is still standing, ringed with grassy pastures and Dutch cows, but we couldn't hear the 'clop of Dutch burghers' shoes' as the guide book suggested. We were pursued by children almost worse than those in Male. We examined the battlements and went down to the beach, then went to the only hotel, another old colonial building, and visited the Dutch church next door. Here

I was pursued by the warden, who finally trapped me in a pew and insisted on giving me the sad story of the community. Apart from the Dutch gravestones there was a good assortment of nineteenth-century British ones, soldiers and the like who had croaked in foreign parts. Just as I was examining some drains being dug in the road outside, with seventeenth-century and later sherds lying in the muddy earth, it came on to rain and we retreated to Speedy. We tried the road south and stopped to buy some pretty lace, and a picnic supper of tomatoes, pineapple, chocolate, bananas and avocado. On the outskirts of Galle we had a fiery lunch of manioc with an exceedingly hot carrot-like dressing, and even hotter tiny dishes of cold mutton curry, and hot vegetables and rissoles, all served with lots of foamy sweet tea in small blue cups. After lunch we drove back to Ambalagoda, buying batiks and a red enamelled Annamese bowl on the way. We swam and got burned in the sun, and later had our picnic supper in the bedroom.

We left the rest house in outrage at the size of the bill and drove on through Galle, and picnicked by the sea and swam. The only bad note were the vulturous crows who hovered over us, delirious at the sight of pineapple and other pickings. It was a pretty beach, with sand and rocks surrounded by palms waving in the high wind. The sea was cleaning up a little, but it was still muddy and agitated from the monsoon. We drove on; more coconut groves, rice paddies, villages of thatched huts strung one after another down the coast; it was very slow because of the people on the road. We got to Tissamaharama, where the tank was full of bathers and wild birds, and the ancient temple across the fields was glaring in the late afternoon sun. The stupa has an improbably large dome, with a square structure on the top and a pinnacle; not good geometry, but peculiar enough to be distinctive. I took a picture of it with a vulturous crow sitting on a cow in the foreground and a withered tree in the distance.

There was also the remains of a torso and a pair of feet, the statue carved with parallel folds so rhythmically as to put the gods of Palmyra to shame. We had tea in the rest house, and toyed with the idea of staying there. As I was screwing the loose number plate back on Speedy we met some Germans, furious at the cost of entering the nature park at Yala, and having decided to stay after all we sped north. It was late afternoon and alarming, as there were forest fires on either side of the road and columns of brown smoke, white at the edges, and a high wind to fan the flames. At Wellawaya there was a rest house with two rooms, one already occupied; we took the other. It was an open bungalow with a tiled roof, the two rooms at either end, with wire netting high on the walls, to keep out …? Our room had three hard beds. There was no electricity and an oil lamp glimmering in the bedroom, and a flickering pressure lamp outside for me to write by.

We went for a walk by the river. The village is in a very eighteenth-century landscape, with blue mountains and every sort of palm and tropical tree in the foreground. In the sluggish pools along the river were evening bathers, and higher up it became very jungly, with odd hooting noises and monkeys crashing about in the trees above. We came back at an upper level, along a watercourse drawn off the river to irrigate fields and the land above.

We woke during the night to thumping, scratching noises but decided that whatever it was, it was outside the Iron Curtain. In the morning when we looked outside a market had already formed in the dusty road, complete with two fortune-tellers, one with a monkey's skull and a lighted taper and a dish full of what looked like stew, and various animal pelts. Judging by the people gathered around, they were taken seriously.

We drove down a bumpy road eastwards to the coast, past a great reservoir, a modern tank. At Kalmunai we found a very beaten-up rest house on an endless golden beach, with the turquoise blue sea turning into dark blue further out. A trio of heavily built German girls came in dripping as we were having a curry lunch. They were disappointed as the sea was too rough to be transparent; they were looking for coral gardens underwater. We drove up the coast in high expectation of finding an even more glamorous rest house in an even more splendid situation. This was a false move, for when we got to Batticoloa it took some time to find the rest house, which was tucked away on a back lagoon beside the oldest Dutch fort on the island, in a less than glamorous spot. As for accommodation, it was not much above last night's standard, and the same price. Water and electricity took turns going off alternately whilst we were there, and buckets and candles substituted for them.

Before it got dark we drove out to the real sea and found an endless sandy beach with scattered palms and a few fishing boats drawn up on the strand. Away from the shore the sea was calm, but close in there was a deep swell with heavy breakers, and a current so strong that it carried you northwards almost at walking pace. Curious Ceylonese mothers and children came and squatted to have a good look at us. Before dusk, I walked round the three landward sides of the Dutch fort. The ground was iron hard, and no one had been doing any digging; the moat was full of cracked mud. The inside of the fort was occupied with modern buildings, perhaps a barracks. There was not a trace of Chinese porcelain anywhere.

We set off north and then inland westwards for Polonnaruwa. We had to stop once to have the silencer fastened back on again, and after I tightened the fan belt the water stopped boiling. We arrived at midday; the rest house was on a cliff above the ancient tank, which was about a mile across, muddy brown and choppy from the high wind. Below us many bathers were winding and re-winding themselves in sheets of trailing cloth. We went first to see the statue of a medieval king south of the tank; carved out of stone he looked very Chinese with his belt knotted like a cloud scroll and long, drooping, curly moustache. Nearby, the ruins with thousands of red bricks, as if Westminster Cathedral and Cadogan Place combined had crumbled into the tropical forest. Again, a stupa with an improbably gigantic solid dome surmounted by a cube and a cone, like a mad art student's balancing game with basic forms, except the dome is too large and the cone is too long. The shrines were set in an inconsequential manner around the base of the hemisphere. Nearby under a tree a boy was playing a pipe to his cobra. He had a very attractive un-Ceylonese face, the head too long and his lips too full. The snake looked at his master in a dazed, uncooperative way; it was not inclined to dance or do anything except uncurl langorously and stare him out.

At the rest house we had another curry lunch. A guest register was produced at the end of the meal, and I started to make fun of the fact that there were Robinsons from High Wycombe and others from Chicago and France, only to realise, to my embarrassment, that the silence to my right meant the Robinsons were sitting at the next table. We went to the museum, and in the dusty clutter found some recently excavated odds and ends sitting on their labels. These included a nice base sherd of white porcelain and three smaller fragments of moulded lids and little bowls, of *qingbai*. Polonnaruwa flourished after the demise of Anuradhapura, and these fragments combined with the evidence of coins from the southern Song found at this site were further proof of contact with the Far East. I washed, drew and photographed the sherds and placed them back on their labels, and left a rather priggish note on the desk addressed to the 'Director/Archaeologist', telling him that I had done this, and that they were interesting, and not to lose them. They were supposed to be from the palace site, so we set off there in the car.

The three little sherds, of tiny bowls and lids for them were of very fine white porcelain and delicately moulded with lotus panels and grooves. The remains of the palace were of more red brick, animated by monkeys scampering around and eating nuts. Again, there had been much restoration with new bricks, and trenches traced the old walls under the trees. Almost as soon as I stepped out of the car, I saw something gleaming in the grey earth; it was another sherd of a tiny lotus bowl. Inspired, we searched around and collected eight pieces altogether, and as had often happened before, the last one we found was the best, lodged in two pieces in the roots of an old tree. This was exactly what had happened once in Male, when I came across the dusty courtyard of a cemetery where I had been looking for sherds to meet Peggy. Incredibly there was the best sherd of all, of carved celadon, lying on the ground between us. The Polonnaruwa sherd was of a bowl with carved and combed decoration on the outside. Although there was no trace of the fourteenth-century blue-and-white bowl that Roland Silva had said was in the museum, instead we had neatly moved backwards in time a couple of centuries or so, and perhaps more profitably, too.

We trailed around the ruins in Speedy Motor on sandy, slithering tracks. We saw more brick ruins and a lotus-shaped bath in a dusty, deserted glade. The trees and stones and dusty nothingness reminded me of Central Park; a New Yorker would feel quite at home here. There was also a temple carved with grinning Fo-dogs or lions and dancers on the outside, and within were the faint traces of elegant wall paintings with a slender Buddha at the altar end. The paintings were of figures against a reddish ground, enlivened with a turquoise green, and reminded me of Pollaiuolo and Signorelli.

Best of all were three gigantic Buddhas, carved, as the guide book would have it, out of 'living rock'. We came across them in a rocky hollow in the forest with more dusty grass, trees and monkeys, and in front a great frangi-pangi tree in full flower. On the left and right two standing figures with a shrine in a recess between them. Further to the right was a reclining Buddha, his elbow dug into a yielding stone cushion and his feet beautifully patterned with flowers on their soles. The tone of all the figures was grained and weathered, and the total effect extraordinary, as if they were carved out of some more lively substance than stone; perhaps 'living rock' was right. The reclining figure is a masterpiece of conceptual sculpture, looking stunning from *every* angle; it was the best thing we had seen so far all summer. I took lots of photographs but would really have liked to have had time to make a drawing, to explore the relationship of the three figures to each other and the rock from which they had been created. But we had to drive on to get to Sigiriya before nightfall.

We continued westwards again along a very bumpy road, then north and east for a few miles until we reached the great rock of Sigiriya. It was evening and the sun caught the stairway leading up the west face, across a sea of green trees. It was the reverse of Polonnaruwa, where nature was extraordinary and used as raw material; here nature was itself, and implanted with alien forms. We checked in at the rest house with lots of French tourists, and planned to climb this strange peak tomorrow. Meanwhile I washed and sorted all the sherds from the day's search, and made notes and drawings to supplement my imperfect memory. Next morning we rose at six to climb Sigiriya, setting out across the fields from the rest house followed by a pack of mangy dogs. A brown one adopted us and spent all its time snapping at the rest. The craggy rock rises abruptly out of the jungle, with enormous boulders at its feet with what seemed like mad staircases of rock-cut steps covering them. They were actually for bonding the foundations of ancient brick walls, long since disappeared. A steep ceremonial staircase led up to the foot of an overhanging gallery, where a dozen or more restored paintings of maidens with globe-like breasts were all that was left of what was once a great gallery of paintings. The walls were also covered with graffiti, old and new, and eventually the staircase emerged on to a platform, halfway up the rock. Here, the stairs for the final ascent led up between two gigantic carved lion's paws. The rest of the climb was over a steeply sloping rock, with ancient steps cut into the smooth surface, with only a rickety iron rail for support. At the very top were the remains of a palace, but it was the view which was compelling. The jungle stretches far away in all directions, with the Kandy range to the south. On the way down, we noticed an overhanging rock painted with polychrome patterns that might have come from Pompeii. Below we walked around the ruined gardens, and then went back to the rest house for breakfast.

We drove on south to Dambulla, parking the car at the bottom of a shelving rock beside the souvenir stalls and lotus stands. We climbed up to the shrine along with many pilgrims, passing armless supplicants and arriving at the temple, where there was a notice asking for funds to electrify the caves. The caves themselves are aligned along a rocky outcrop, with a platform outside with a view of the jungle, chiefly inhabited with fertile monkeys – there were lots of babies everywhere. The mothers were busily engaged in picking nits from their offspring. Inside the caves, the entrances opened up on different parts of reclining Buddhas, and there were rows and rows of identical seated Buddhas, like some great extended family. They were all mustard yellow, once shiny and now dusty, picked out in other colours. Again, some were carved from the actual rock, the cave created in fact by carving around the statue. One reclining figure with his elbow on a stone cushion was so realistically painted that the cushions looked like a dirty inflated plastic pillow. The undulating roof was painted with rows and rows of Buddhas and a chequered pattern which the natural formation of the rock made look like a billowing canopy. Various specially sacred spots had strips of coloured rags and semi-transparent curtains hung in front of them. At this moment two barefoot girls ran into the caves, ran all around and then ran out at top speed.

We left after donating at least a lamp bulb or two for the electrification project, and as we descended met pilgrims of all ages climbing up towards us, carrying peeled white lotuses. The lotuses were sold at the bottom of the rocky slope, all green and shut up, like simplified artichokes. We set off again, this time on a specific mission, to Anuradhapura.

Anuradhapura is the most important site in Sri Lanka, stretching for miles through the jungle. With a prehistoric past, it came into its own in the fifth century BC with the arrival of Buddhism and swiftly developed into the capital, with an economy based on the successful irrigation of the northern dry zone of the island with a sophisticated network of canals and reservoirs, or tanks. It not only became the religious centre but also the economic focus of the island, and supplied the capital for trade, both with the coastal towns but also abroad. This economic growth led to large-scale building activity, of palaces, stupas, temples and monastic structures of all sorts. However, the prosperity came to an abrupt end in the tenth century AD with the Chola invasion from India of northern Sri Lanka. This completely disrupted the carefully balanced agricultural economy, the irrigation canals and tanks were laid waste, and the capital moved south-east to Polonnaruwa. Anuradhapura never regained its former status, but from the nineteenth century onwards attracted the attention of numerous archaeologists, including H. C. P. Bell who established an archaeological rest house and museum on the site.

This housed not only material from Anuradhapura, but also from other sites in the northern area, which was the real reason for our visit. In the museum were three pieces of Chinese ware, which together with Chinese coins had been excavated at Yapahuwa, in 1911. These consisted of two white-ware bowls and a celadon one, and interested me in particular as the site was only inhabited from the early thirteenth century until it was destroyed in AD 1284. Thus Yapahuwa provides a neat *terminus ante quem* for the Chinese bowls in question. But when we arrived, every move we made in Speedy Motor to get to the sacred area at the centre of the site was defeated by barricades of stones across the road. It seemed as if a siege was taking place, but it was only a siege against the incursion of vehicles, for anything else could easily circumnavigate the barriers. At last we located the museum, which luckily turned out to be outside the sacred precincts. I presented my papers from the Archaeological Commission in

Colombo, giving me permission to draw and photograph anything in sight. This provoked consternation, for it was Sunday afternoon and although the museum was functioning the Director was not. There then took place a lengthy circular conversation with the six meek museum officials who were on duty, and a not-so-meek hag. Eventually they came round to my initial suggestion, that one of them should go with me to the house of the absent Director and pry the key out of him. On our way through the suburban development of Anuradhapura, we met the Director's servant riding a bicycle in the opposite direction, carrying a shopping bag. He leapt into the car, leaving our companion from the museum with the bicycle and the bag.

Off we went to his master's house, a modest, dusty-curtained bungalow well out of town. In he went. After a longish wait he reappeared, to say that master was away, in town, and his wife didn't know when he would be back. I sent him back to tell the wife it was now 1.30, and I would return at 5, to know whether or not I could start work tomorrow promptly at 8, or else I would be obliged to leave. There was an even longer wait. He returned after conferring with the wife, who had now mysteriously assumed his master's powers behind those dingy curtains. He now told me that if we could find the Assistant Director, even further into the wilderness of Anuradhapura, we could work today. I noted a pair of white muslin trousers on the washing line. After another lengthy wait, they were snatched off the washing line, and I knew it was going to be all right. The Director appeared and back we all went to the museum, where there was much laughter and shrieks of pleasurable relief all round.

The cases were unlocked and the pots produced; our ranks had now swollen to seven. I spent the next couple of hours in the upper gallery of the museum, drawing and photographing and making all those dull manoeuvres such work entails. This drew much mirth from the seven, every move I made first being commented on by the hag, and then by the appreciative six. I could have cheerfully kicked them all in the ankles. But the compensation was the bowls themselves, which turned out to be intact and quite splendid examples of their kind. The celadon was particularly interesting, for it was the same Song type as the earliest celadon piece in the collection in Topkapi Sarayi in Istanbul. William Willetts had already made the suggestion that this bowl is in fact the famous Bowl Relic, the supposed alms bowl of the Buddha, which disappeared from the shrine in Kandy at that date. His theory is that the Bowl Relic like the Tooth Relic (which is actually a crocodile tooth) was a substitution. In any case, this bowl would fit very well with Marco Polo's description of the Bowl in AD 1293, which he says is of 'very beautiful green porphyry'. The Chinese coins, incidentally, which were also found at Yapahuwa, ranged in date from AD 996 to 1225. Besides the three Chinese bowls, there were also many other interesting finds in the storeroom of the museum, including Islamic sherds and lustre, and Chinese Tang dynasty splashed earthenware from Changsha, all from Tirukketisvaram (that is, Mantai). I galloped through the material, snapping left and right, and finished only ten minutes past closing time. It was ten past four, and I had a splitting headache.

For the cocktail hour, we set off for Mihintale. There was another reason for this detour, for this was the site from which two ninth-century Islamic turquoise glazed pots had been excavated, now in the Colombo Museum. As I was to find out later, similar complete jars had been found in a dated tomb of Lia Hua, who died in AD 930. So the pots from Sri Lanka were a sort of halfway house, on the long maritime route to the east. I also wanted to see the processional staircase at Mihintale, a nineteenth-century watercolour of which I had admired in the museum, in a sort of Roberts oriental style. The reality was even better, without the romantic tropicalia and frangi-pangi ('temple flowers') all the way up instead. Pilgrims drifted up and down the shallow steps; like all wide treads, they were not easy to mount, and we drifted with them. We were befriended by a barefoot girl who spoke remarkably good English and knew the site backwards. It transpired that her father was the night guardian at the top, and she wanted to become a doctor; she earned pocket money for extra books by guiding the likes of us. We went with her halfway up, then she and the others went to see another temple, and I made a circular swing past a sexy, rampant lion really to lure a beggar at the top of the steps to have his picture taken against the melting jungle landscape. This particular beggar had one leg missing and a metal replacement; he was bearded and otherwise whole, and might have come straight out of Muybridge. I made mystical passes over him to try to convey the beauty of my concept, but he had no objection to having his photo taken, he didn't seem to mind. We went back down the staircase and saw the remains of the hospital from which the turquoise jars had been excavated. We then went on to Medawachchiya, where we stayed in the rest house where we had stopped for tea, just a month ago. The lights flickered and failed, but came on just in time for dinner, a quickly cooked curry put together in the kitchen from chopped vegetables and coconut.

Next day we were on the road to Mannar, our final destination in Sri Lanka, from which we would take the ferry back to India again. On the way we stopped at a potters' village, with thatched huts and hundreds of black and shiny cooking pots in traditional shapes. It occurred to me that the so-called carinated metal form might not necessarily be metallic in origin; it could simply be the easiest way to join the two separate halves of a vessel. A couple of miles before we got to Mannar, we turned off the main road to the coast, westwards across the salty flats. We came to a village called Vankalai, dominated by a Catholic church, and drove speculatively south from there looking for an equivalent site to Mantai, which Roland Silva said existed somewhere in that vicinity. We couldn't find it and gave up, and I drove off the road to turn around. I looked down and there was pottery everywhere.

This became even more interesting when I picked up a shell fragment and it turned out to be Chinese porcelain. This was all on the east side of the road, and the sea was a couple of hundred yards to the west. We tracked down to the sea, but there was nothing to be seen but some fishermen far away, wading across an inlet. But on the way back to the car, on the edge of a thorny thicket, there were bumps and erosions full of pottery, mostly reddish earthenware but with enough porcelain to make things interesting. And there was an earthenware rim sherd of exactly the type from the bottom of my little pit in the garden of the Sultan's palace in Male, and pieces of white glazed ware like those from there too.

The consequences of this minor discovery that afternoon on the way to Mannar dictated the shape of my researches in the decade to come. When I returned to Sri Lanka a couple of years later, to make a more detailed survey of the coastline of India and Sri Lanka, systematically looking for ports mentioned in either Chinese or Islamic medieval texts, I found myself in Colombo once more. I particularly wanted to return to Mantai, which I had realised was of paramount importance as far as long-distance maritime trade between the east and west was concerned. However, all the archaeological staff were busy, and more importantly had commandeered the departmental vehicles in order to attend a ceremony at the site of Pandubas Nuvara, where the recently elected Prime Minister was to engage in a symbolic act of ploughing a field. This was the revival of an ancient custom, and was meant to encourage the peasants to go back to the land, rather than seek the delights of city life. The presence of the entire archaeological department was required, and this meant my proposed survey of Mannar and the north coast was off. In desperation I telephoned a young friend who was an architect and also an amateur archaeologist; he told me he didn't have a car, but if I liked we could take the train to Jaffna, and see what we could do from there.

The next day we arrived in Jaffna, on the north-east peninsular of the island. Jaffna was also the centre of the

Tamil community in Sri Lanka, and the focus for the oncoming struggle for independence which was to lead to a bloody civil war; there had already been riots in Colombo. My architect friend had showed me Chinese sherds he had picked up in Jaffna some months ago, when he had gone to buy building sand on the nearby Kayts island, in order to restore the home of a Tamil client, an engineer by profession. All three of us drove out to the site in the dusk, only to find that it had been completely denuded of sand and there was nothing left. At this point a Tamil boy on a bicycle asked us what we were after, and on being told we were looking for Chinese pottery, he said he knew where there was lots of it. With nothing to lose, we followed him on his bicycle in the car. He led us down to the sea, and abandoning both car and bicycle trekked down into the sand dunes. It was now almost dark, and stumbling around in the dunes where he said other labourers had been digging for sand, I heard the unmistakable sound of breaking pottery; we were actually treading on sherds of Chinese porcelain. Gathering up what we could carry back to the car, we returned to Jaffna and electric light, to examine what we had found.

We had stumbled on a whole heap of Chinese *qinqbai* dishes. Of translucent white porcelain with finely engraved and combed floral designs, they were of the Song dynasty, of the first half of the twelfth century. We returned to the site early next morning, to find the labourers had dug away half of a whole hoard of Chinese pots, of which the other half was clearly showing in the section of their trench, about a metre below the surface of the sand dunes. In exasperation they had thrown the Chinese pots which had befouled their nice clean building sand on the top of the dune. It was an extraordinary sight. I decided we must do something about the rest, and with the help of students from Jaffna, who were stuck at home because of the rioting in Colombo, we mounted an impromptu dig. During the next few days, we uncovered the rest of the deposit and carefully recorded its disposition. There were thousands of sherds, and often parts of the same vessel dispersed all over the same site. There was no trace of settlement, so I came to the conclusion that it was an abandoned shipment, perhaps on its way from China to the west. Maybe it had befallen an accident at sea, and the sailors had simply sorted out the whole pieces from the broken vessels and left the debris behind. Nor did it appear to have been consciously buried; the sand seemed to have naturally drifted on top of the sherds.

Having gathered the material, there was now the problem of what to do with it. Back in Jaffna, the government agent very kindly lent us the King's House, the main residence in the old Dutch fort. I stayed there, and we had a vast room with plenty of tables in order to sort out the pottery and try to piece together again as much as possible of it. First of all we had to wash it; we filled the large tub in the adjoining bathroom three times over, and it took two boys three days to wash it all. There were over six thousand fragments, and we then began the monumental task of sorting them all out. We purchased the entire supply of glue in Jaffna, and with the help of more students from the university spent ten days engaged in a gigantic jigsaw puzzle. At the end of it, we had identified more than four hundred vessels, of thirty-five different types. After we had finished drawing and photographing the material, we transferred it all to the little museum in Jaffna.

It was quite an experience being all alone in the Dutch fort in Jaffna, many years later to become the focus of the Tamil resistance and bombarded by the Sri Lankan army. The King's House had been used in colonial times as a residence for the British Commissioner when he was on circuit, and poking around I found all sorts of table linen and napkins, and a toaster, very much in the style of Heals of the fifties, evidence of the transient imperial presence. Even more interesting, I found the whole complex described by Leonard Wolff in the first volume of his autobiography; he had been the local agent in Jaffna, and used to play tennis in the fort. And one night, sleeping in the room where we were mending the pottery, I had a very odd experience.

I woke up in the middle of the night, to find I had been levitated from my bed, and was being dashed from one side of the room to the other at ceiling height, then to the door, and then back to my bed, where I was finally dumped. Whether a dream or not, it was so vividly real that I not only wrote the experience down in my diary but also described it in a letter home. Some years later, I read the autobiography of an American ambassador to Sri Lanka, and was amazed to find he had a similar experience when staying in the fort on circuit. He was told that there was a ghostly explanation; apparently a maiden had been raped by the Dutch and her body thrown down a well in the garden (there was just such a well off the kitchen), and she came back regularly to haunt visitors.

Back in Colombo, word had got out about our discovery and I became a minor celebrity. It was even reported in the local press: 'Chinese pottery of the Sing dynasty found in a sand dune', which sounded rather musical. More to the point, it endeared me to Roland Silva, the Archaeological Commissioner, who was convinced that I had some sort of diviner's skill when it came to detecting antiquities. He asked me if I would like to come back again next year, and I said I would like to investigate the little site near Vankalai. Having obtained his permission, I then went about seeking funds to excavate and an archaeologist more experienced than I to supervise the work. In the event, we came back in 1979, this time with Peggy and Andy, and an old friend, Diana Kirkbride. Diana was a famous prehistorian, trained by Kathleen Kenyon like myself at Jericho in the fifties, who had then gone on to excavate a neolithic site at Petra, which added yet another important link in the chain of the history of mankind.

The site was on the edge of a lagoon, linked by a narrow channel to the sea, and I had lured Peggy with photographs of the lagoon and some propaganda about how idyllic it was all going to be. In fact, it was less than idyllic; the lagoon turned out to be only nine inches deep, with a thick layer of evil-smelling mud below. On the one occasion when I swam in the ocean, I found I was not alone; there was a sea serpent, looking very much like I imagined the Loch Ness monster and about fifty feet long, undulating in the waves. I got out fast. As for the site, we had to clear part of the jungle to set up our tents. This infuriated the local pack of Lanka monkeys, about a hundred of them, who regarded it as territorial intrusion. I saw one up a palm tree actually shaking his fist angrily at us. On another occasion, the whole pack got between us and the camp when Peggy and I were out for a walk along the lagoon, and we barely made it back safely.

The tents had built-in linings (they had been meant for refugees, supplied by the United Nations) and were incredibly hot and sticky inside. I well remember a visit from the next Archaeological Commissioner, Siran Deraniyagala, whom I offered the hospitality of a spare tent. He took one look at it, and instead had his servant set up a camp bed with fresh white linen and pillows under a nearby tree; we were envious. Added to our misery, there was no fresh water, which had to be trucked in from Vankalai every day by Peggy and a local lad whose car we hired. The Sinhalese cook was not only bad, but had a venomous disposition. The workmen were lackadaisical, largely the result of hangovers from the lethal *raki*, palm toddy consumed the night before. Diana got cross at what she considered my unprofessional organisation of the whole enterprise; not, she made clear, what she was used to. In the end she only deigned to speak to Andy, who was then seven, and with whom she became quite good friends. Andy had his own cross to bear, as he was out of school, and we arranged for him to have lessons in Vankalai with the local Catholic priest. There was nothing wrong with that, as the lessons never materialised and they used to have tea and biscuits instead. But the indignity was getting there and back, for he had to be transported on the back of a bicycle ridden by a ten-year-old village girl. Finally, the repeating alarm clock given us by a friend in Chicago (where we were by now living, after leaving Beirut as a result of the civil war), began to get strange messages back from the jungle every time it went off. Something out there, apparently, was trying to mate with it.

In short, it was a nightmare dig. Archaeologically it was also singularly unrewarding, as the low mound covered with scrub jungle had plenty of pottery on top of it, but little below; and what was below was of compacted mud brick the consistency of concrete. This only responded to massive pickaxe blows, and fine trowelling was out of the question. Not that this mattered, as there was barely any definable stratigraphy, and even Diana gave up. But the finds were interesting, and we came to the conclusion from the imported Chinese and Islamic wares that this was a little settlement, which lasted perhaps fifty years or so, at the beginning of the twelfth century, and more or less contemporary with the Chinese hoard on Kayts island, for which there were some direct parallels. There was, for instance, a base sherd of Chinese *qingbai* with exactly similar carved and combed decoration. There was a preponderance of local earthenware bowls with interior incised lines, used for husking rice. So our final verdict was that this was a village which had briefly flourished in the period after the collapse of the economy of northern Sri Lanka as the result of the Chola invasion a century earlier. This modest attempt at reviving the agricultural economy had failed, and the land reverted to the jungle. The village had, however, been prosperous enough during its brief existence to be able to purchase both imported Islamic and Chinese wares, which demonstrated an interesting link with the outside world.

Pondering on all this, I suddenly realised that this combination of three cultures on the same site – Chinese, Islamic and local – had much wider implications. In this case we were using the foreign imports to date the site in general terms. However, the reverse could be equally valid, for at the great city sites such as Anuradhapura and Polonnaruwa, buildings were dateable from epigraphic evidence; and pottery associated with such buildings, even if it was only local ware, could by extrapolation be used to date coastal sites such as the one we had dug. More important still, if one could link the pottery from Anuradhapura with its dependant port at Mantai, then the Mantai material could be used in turn to date all the ceramic material from both ends of Asia. It is surprising, but a fact, that the chronology of both Islamic and Chinese pottery was quite loose, and lacking systematic and scientific excavation of sites in the Islamic world and China, Mantai could play a most important role.

But, alas Mantai was the province of the Archaeological Commission, and there was little chance of digging there. Except, the last night I was in Colombo after we had wrapped up Vankalai, Roland Silva asked me when I was coming back to dig again. I replied that the only site I was interested in was Mantai, and that I knew that this was out of the question. No it isn't, he said, for Dr Raja da Silva, the Commissioner, had his birthday yesterday. As a civil servant, there is mandatory retirement at sixty, so he will no longer be excavating Mantai. He suggested that I put in an application for the site, and this is exactly what I did. I began to excavate at Mantai in 1980, and was lucky enough to have three seasons before the civil war broke out with a vengeance in 1984. But that is another story, and like the site itself, now discreetly buried in the jungle of time.

8

INDIA ONCE MORE

IT WAS THE END OF AUGUST when we checked in to the rest house in Mannar for the second time, on our way to catch the ferry back to India. It was still in its flotsam state, and we got to know it well in the years to come when we dug at Mantai, and it became the only weekly respite from the rigours of the site, for being close to the holy Hindu temple we were supposed to be strictly vegetarian and drink was absolutely forbidden. Ultimately, the rest house was a victim of the scourge of Mannar by the Sri Lankan army in 1984; I am afraid it is little regretted in my memories. This time, there was only one room for the four of us, hot, sticky and peeling pink walls. There was more curry for lunch, and our friend from a month ago materialised, Mohammed Farouk, from the filling station opposite. After eating we set off for our second visit to the ancient kingdom of Mantai. The two young men from the archaeological commission whom we had met the first time round were there, digging a neat L-shaped trench metre by metre downwards. They had saved some Chinese sherds, and we set off on a tour of the site together, Peggy lingering behind, and as I hoped, picking up all she could discreetly. There was lots of porcelain, and brilliant blue or turquoise glazed Islamic sherds; they must have once competed with the refined but duller Chinese wares. We made a circuit of the site, which was enormous, with a horseshoe-shaped double moat around it and a shallow tank on the south side. It was almost completely covered with scrub jungle, and some bumps on the north side suggested there might be a gateway. Everywhere there was pottery lying on the surface; I longed to be alone to do a real search, unimpeded by my two enthusiastic companions. They told me about two snakes which had been killed when they cleared part of the bush, and promised me the skin of one of them. We returned by the temple, a modern construction now in the middle of the site, and surrounded by a little village of thatched huts. They told me that they had found a *lingam*, which was now installed in the temple, a gaily painted affair with a truncated pyramid of gods and goddesses, and the elaborately carved juggernaut used for festivals housed in a sort of thatched garage in the precincts.

We photographed part of the Arabic stone inscription I had seen on our first visit, and they suggested the rest of it might as easily be in Anuradhapura as Colombo; I wish I had thought to ask about it the day before. We put all our sherds in a plastic bag and set off in search of the promised snake skin, which had been given to a friend, Peggy slowly following us in the car, rather like a hearse. We came to a little hut behind a bungalow filled with young men. Sit down, they said; I sat. The skin was produced from a dark recess, and unrolled; it was mottled and at least seven feet long. Would I like it if they cleaned it? Yes, I said; I should have perhaps politely said no, for there was lots of laughter and goodbyes and off we sped *without* the skin. I think the owner understandably didn't really want to part with it.

Back in the rest house I washed the day's finds and set them out to dry, and Mohammed appeared and we had a very interesting conversation. He is quite happy in Mannar with his family; maybe he will be transferred to Kandy. He doesn't like Colombo and city life, doesn't drink or smoke, but does like reading and playing tennis. And, I think, chatting up everyone who passes through the rest house. (But he is such an educated creature that it is impossible to take offence.) The conversation turned to scientific archaeology, Ceylonese history and maritime trade and all sorts of other topics. He was remarkably well informed, and at that time I wondered if he might not be a sort of subtle government spy, to report on travellers, which I could see might be a profession not without interest. (Years later I learned the truth about Mohammed; he wasn't just working as a petrol pump attendant, he owned it; and he was in fact the leader of the Muslim community in Mannar, for whom he was responsible. He had a particularly nasty time during the ensuing civil war, when the entire town was burned to the ground by the army, and when last heard of was living as a refugee in Colombo.) Mohammed told us a scathing story about last night's crop of visitors at the rest house, which included two Swiss who had been around the past six months, trying to educate the local peasantry to appreciate how they were being exploited by the landowners. As Mohammed said, it was impossible to convince the Swiss that perhaps they were not being exploited at all. They had left today for the same boat that we were catching tomorrow. He also told us to look out for a *manara* (the Arabic for 'lighthouse') about seven or eight miles up the road.

Next morning, we didn't see the lighthouse, but arrived in good time to catch the ferry at Telemannar, at 7am. Already there was a large gathering of Tamils being repatriated to India, and assorted foreigners. We spotted the Swiss, in a scarlet VW, both wearing baggy cotton pants, she with a top and he with an orange shirt; they were thin-lipped, long-haired and wearing rimless spectacles. After an eternity we were loaded on to the boat with Speedy, and set off once more across Adam's Bridge. I questioned one of the officers about the straits, and he told me that they were very shallow, with a string of underwater reefs, and only negotiable by fishing boats; there was no deeper channel that he knew of, and boats of any size could only reach one side or the other, or sail south of Ceylon altogether. So all the trade must have passed through Mannar, and this would account for the growth and importance of Mantai as a point of trans-shipment on the eastern side of Adam's Bridge, as well as a point of contact with the Indian subcontinent to the north.

We arrived at Rameswaram late in the afternoon, and out came the tug with three boats in tow. On the first one was the chief car loader from our previous trip, who was very friendly and told us the cars would be unloaded in the morning. When we got to the customs shed, the nicest of the Negoomeera brothers was there and embraced me, laughing as usual. This time his mirth was about a kooky American girl, who had reappeared like us after a trip round Sri Lanka. Apparently when she had left India she had a typewriter declared on her passport, which had not accompanied her on her side trip, and the customs naturally enquired about its whereabouts. She informed Negoomeera (I am not sure how) that she could not answer any questions verbally, as she was in direct mental contact with her Swami, and could only reply in writing. Thus ensued an extraordinary game with papers and pencils, the customs supplying written questions, and after she had cast her eyes Swami-wise, she giving written answers. The Swami was apparently quite law abiding, as he agreed she should leave a largish sum of money on deposit for the missing typewriter, which could be reclaimed on her return. We had coincided with her re-entry, swathed in trailing scarves and lots of beads, and a distant stare. I wished we had known about her on the boat. I last saw her beside the fattest of the Negoomeera brothers, the financial branch of the family, seated and casting her eyes once more upwards and Swami-wise. She must then have dematerialised, with or without the deposit, for we never saw her again.

It was inevitable that the Swiss should make an entry into our lives instead. I had already told him that the Negoomeera's agent was looking after our formalities and would look after his too. He came up to tell me he had brought pressure to bear and made the agent agree to unload tonight instead of tomorrow morning. I was cross because it was almost dark and I did not want to land Speedy in the night. But he had already stamped on the nice Negoomeeras and they had good-naturedly agreed. Except that it meant we now had to wait as well, as both cars had to be unloaded at once, and we could not go to the Railway Retiring Rooms and Rameswaram station, which as soon as we had landed had been booked for us by Negoomeera's boy, who had brought us the key. So we were stuck in the customs, with a great many repatriated Tamils being assimilated back into the bosom of Mother India. The Negoomeeras were nice as nice could be, but even they could hardly advance matters any faster. We waited hours, then finally Speedy arrived and I drove her off the lurching boat on to the sandy beach. There was more paperwork, and we were so tired by the time we were finished we were almost past retiring at all. But as we did, the Swiss crept up in their nasty VW camper and parked in the station yard (as usual, for nothing) and shut themselves in for the night.

Next morning I rather uncharitably hoped they had locked themselves in for good and asphyxiated, for they were unusually slow to emerge. I had already been to the Station Master's office and done most of my formalities, when the door of the camper slid open and they came out with two wickerwork stools, to munch away cheaply beside their scarlet beast. I was glad to see someone had given them a nasty bash on the front left side. We went off to see the temple in Rameswaram, picking up some milky coffee and a scrap of breakfast on the way. When we arrived at the entrance, the temple elephant had just been let out for the morning, and as I tried to take its likeness, to my embarrassment it shat about a hundred kilos and peed like a fire hydrant. I held my exposure for a quieter moment.

The entrance to the temple, which Kathy had identified from a guide as 'the finest example of evolved Dravidian architecture', in fact had a new entrance finished in 1972. It was beautifully carved and rather amazing to know such skills still exist. After we had shed our shoes, we went inside the temple, and met the relieved elephant, now comfortably stabled with its guard in the entrance gallery among the statues. Andy would *not* respond to the invitation to have his picture taken sitting on the elephant, which was a pity as it could have been a remarkably surrealist image. He could not relate the elephant to the one he had so clamoured to mount in the Colombo zoo, nor indeed to our own stuffed elephant which we had at home in Beirut. The temple had lengthy corridors, and we were allowed to see nothing else. Stalls were just opening up inside the temple complex – it was still early – and we bought baskets and toys and I resisted buying a bunch of detachable wooden bananas. But I did get a tinted picture of lovely ladies swimming ecstatically in space, around a *lingam*.

We went back to the Railway Retiring Rooms, to repack and deliver the car to the ramp leading on to the train. The Swiss crept round the corner a few seconds later, and we met once more, in the Station Master's office (Package Department). They filled their forms in first, and my guesses about their stinginess were confirmed when I heard them ask for 'low-west glass tickets'. For some snivelling extra sum we went first class, to my satisfaction not having to face them for an hour and a half across a tiny carriage.

Whilst we were waiting for the train at Rameswaram, a grey-eyed, thin, bespectacled Frenchman came up to show us his baby tortoise. It was a star tortoise, which a friendly Chinese in Trincomalee had given him as a parting present. He had been three months in India and Ceylon, and was going back to Delhi and Paris with his friends and his tortoise. Talking with him gave me the faintest shiver of Autumn, which was strange here where such a season doesn't exist. It must have been the mention of Paris, or perhaps his pale, slightly sallow French complexion, or maybe just the way he spoke English in the way only the French do. But it reminded me of France at just this time of year, and in particular when I had been in Brittany twenty years ago, when the leaves shivered in the main square of a small town. One could detect the faintest deepening of green to gold, and the first straggling leaves wrenched off by a light breeze. It was time to return to the capital, to Paris where the rain doesn't matter in the boulevards, to cafes, to lights, things to do and people to talk with interminably. It was as if the town was a magnet, drawing the leaves off all the trees in the countryside, hinting that the time had come to return. It was strange to have the same sensation at the southern tip of India.

We rumbled across the bridge from the island to the mainland, and landed at Mandapam. I was just remarking how I hoped an infinity of Indian children had been sick over the Swiss in 'low-west glass', when they passed by and hopefully heard. They re-passed a few minutes later down the tracks, and shouted 'it's ready' at me; I shouted back 'good', and sat tight. Andy and I sauntered down the other side of the train and when we arrived at our leisure, found them panting at the wheel of the camper and ready to go – except Speedy had to go, first. We went down the ramp, the railway shunters wanting tips. I asked them how much the Swiss had coughed up; their eyes rolled to heaven, for just as at Rameswaram, the Swiss were against tips in any circumstance. Perhaps they felt it further added to the exploitation of the poor. But they had the last word, when I discovered the back of my luggage rack buckled up into itself, done at some stage by their eager, armoured camper.

We had a delicious and rather expensive lunch in a hovel in Mandapam called the Hotel Michael, where we ate *sans* cutlery off palm leaves for the first time. First, you washed your leaf down with water, and then a ladle-full of fish curry and a spoonful of a spinach-like vegetable were laid on the leaf, with some onion and tomato condiment and pieces of delicious, freshly fried fish. Andy was quite perturbed as he was at the stage in his education when we were trying at home to convince him it was *not* good manners to eat bacon with your fingers, and here we all were scooping it up with our hands. A very pretty lady in a smart sari opposite us was shovelling her lunch down at top speed with never a splash. It was all the more difficult for us, for unlike the Arab world where you can squeeze rice and meat into a relatively stable mass to pop into your mouth, here the food was intractably liquid. After we had cleaned ourselves up under a nearby tap we had hot sweet foamy tea to finish with, and paid the extortionate bill (R. 15.75) with mixed emotions, as it was honestly one of the best meals we have had, admittedly in the most squalid surroundings. And for Andy it was another stage marked up on the learning curve.

On the road again, I cleared the usual crowd of fifty-plus who had gathered around Speedy by holding out my hand and asking for alms for looking. This time we were heading for a pearl-divers village called Tuticorin, but when we arrived it turned out to be a rather large commercial shipping town, no pearl divers in sight. To get there we had at first got lost in the plains of southern India, with specks of rain and the threat of distant storms. There were factories and great piles of blinding white salt on the flats, and brilliant turquoise birds of strange shape wheeling around slowly in the darkening sky. In town, we found the Government Circuit House; it was empty and luckily for once we got a suite and had some thin tea. We went shopping for gin, and when we returned we were spotted by the staff on the steps, carrying the Cholrox upstairs in an empty whisky bottle. In the morning there was a further contretemps over the tea, for this time instead of the pot of hot water we had asked for so we could make our own, they had infused it with their own brand. This time it was too strong, but after a pilgrimage downstairs we eventually got a palatable brew. We drove back through Tuticorin, and then rather too fast south to the tip of India, at Cape Comorin, which did the silencer in again.

Here the sand was two colours, one brown and the other plain dirty. The sea was choppy and dirty too, and a Hindu shrine on a rock did not look very attractive. There was a memorial to Mahatma Gandhi, a fancy exercise in reinforced concrete emblazoned on the front with a hand loom. It was very weathered and there was nothing to see inside except a slab upon which his remains had finally rested. It was all rather disappointing, and after a coffee by the wayside we set off for Nagercoil, where we changed travellers' cheques and found an expensive and unprepossessing room for the night.

We bought a picnic of tomatoes, onion and rolls, and soft drinks and tangerines, and ate them in the forecourt of a seventeenth-century Kerala palace. It was designed very much in Chinese style and had beautiful mirror-black plastered floors, ingenious teak screens, and three four-poster beds in Portuguese style. The dining hall, which looked large enough to feed a thousand, was very simple and elegant. In an upper gallery there were pictures of gods and goddesses in almost eighteenth-century style, as if Nicola Manucci might have passed by. The gardens of carefully swept gravel and potted plants, the teak carving and the lacquer finishes made one speculate if this might not be the tradition from which the mosques and tombstones in the Maldives sprang.

I was sad to find my light meter had also been a victim of our fast and bumpy drive. Luckily I had an older second one, else my pictures would have come to an end for the rest of our journey. After lunch, another victim was a boy on a bicycle carrying a load of fish, whom I crashed into as he unexpectedly swerved out of a village side street into the main road. Luckily again he was unharmed, and I straightened out his handlebars and set him on his way with his fishy load. I got back into the car just in time, and drove off as an angry gang of villagers began to close in on us, for whatever pickings were to be had. The children and crowds in general were impossible here, and viciously inquisitive. Driving up the coast road was a nightmare of evading children, animals, bicycles, cows and the thundering Tata buses, aiming straight at one and forcing you off the shoulder and into the ditch. We arrived at

Trivandrum having missed Kovalam on the way, so we drove back down the coast road. Kovalam was a sad disappointment. The sea was rough and dirty, adjectives which could be equally well applied to the hotel operators. We found a government bungalow on a superb bluff, but both its rooms were booked, and nothing we could do would prevail the servants to make space for us. So we returned to Trivandrum and at last found a hotel, after trying all the rest houses, which were full because of an All-India Congress of Headmasters of Secondary Schools. We didn't see any headmasters, but Trivandrum seemed to be fairly hot politically, for there were speeches in the streets and I absentmindedly cut a swathe with Speedy through a procession of protesting bank clerks. The hotel was expensive, for a bad room by the receptionist's desk, and the curry tasted suspiciously like one has at home.

We set off to do something about the car. We found Stones Garage, run by a strong silent man whom I at first thought was another customer. He fixed the silencer and the front bumper, not without some effort, and his mechanic came for a trial ride with us to see if he could diagnose the knocking noise. The unsatisfactory verdict was that it was not anything to do with the engine, but probably some kind of metal fault in the superstructure. Crossing our fingers and with the address of someone competent in Coimbatore, off we went. But not before we had checked out the local museum, and found an early Yuan celadon *guan*, a large celadon dish with a ribbed cavetto and a lotus at the centre, a large Swatow jar painted with *qilin* above breaking waves, and a Swatow bowl enamelled in red and green with a monster in underglaze blue at the centre, and most surprising of all, a large Tz'u Chou vase painted in brownish black on a cream ground with dragons and phoenixes.

The countryside was now lush like the coast of Ceylon, but the road truly maddening. What with the unpredictable knock to occupy one's imagination, the pedestrians, suicidal cyclists and the murderous oncoming Tata buses took all one's energy to defy. We cruised into Quilon at a more leisurely pace, and after one misdirection found the tourist bungalow, a steeply-roofed country house within a Palladian gateway, across a dishevelled lawn full of grazing cows. It was, as usual, 'fully booked' with totally invisible guests, just as it was at Kovalam and Trivandrum. No amount of argument would make the manager relent, although he clearly had strings of empty rooms. We came to the conclusion this was a move to force tourists to stay in the new hotels. It was almost as difficult to get into the guest house opposite the railway station. We did though, and dislodged about a million mosquitos from the two ancient beds. We lit rings of Chinese coils around them and set off to find old Quilon.

First we drove south of the town across an inland canal; here there was a long curving beach with steeply shelving sand, but no trace of a natural port. We made our way to the headland at the north end of the beach, where we found the remains of a two-storeyed fort and a quantity of pottery, mostly sixteenth century and later. Where the sea had eroded the edge of the land a couple of pieces of celadon testified to an earlier occupation. This was once the great port for ships from east and west and, according to George Hourani, the furthest point to which Chinese vessels traded. Quilon was known to the Arabs as *Kulam Male*, and was the landfall for ships sailing directly across the Indian Ocean from the Red Sea and the Persian Gulf. From at least the first century AD, the Arabs discovered the secret of the monsoons and sailing direct rather than hugging the coast from one port to another. The development of this system was the foundation of the maritime trade between the civilisations of Asia, China, India and the Islamic world. From the goods traded back and forth there are many records, and great fortunes were made by Arab entrepreneurs and shipowners making the long sea voyage to China and back again. Of the goods themselves, there is little trace on excavations in the monsoon belt of perishable, organic materials. What does remain are ceramics and glass, and these are the best evidence for trade and cultural contacts. The exception to the rule are ports in more arid areas, such as Quseir al-Qadim on the Egyptian coast of the Red Sea. Here the dry climate has preserved wood and leather, and even written documents and Indian textiles, as well as the more durable pottery and metalwork.

We also have the evidence of those who travelled, who wrote down what they saw. Sulayman al-Sirafi about AD 750 gives a vivid account of the early days of Arab navigation, and in the medieval period we have the famous record of the Venetian traveller, Marco Polo. But perhaps even more interesting is that of the Arab traveller, Ibn Battuta, who journeyed from his native Morocco to the Near East, Mecca and Central Asia, then down into India and the Maldives and ultimately to China, at the beginning of the fourteenth century. He not only describes the manufacture of Chinese porcelain at just about the moment that blue-and-white was introduced, but also makes the intriguing remark that it was exported all over China, but also to India and the Maghrib, i.e. Morocco. Clearly, the bulk of Chinese porcelain travelled by sea, but recent research has shown that some of it also travelled along the Central Asian trade routes, from Jingdezen in south central China where it was made, up to Beijing and Sian, Inner Mongolia and across the Gobi desert to the Tien Shan range, then down into the plain of the Oxus, Samarkand and Bokhara, to Persia and the west.

The ultimate destination for much of the trade from the Far East and India from the Roman period onwards was the Mediterranean. But with the arrival of the Portuguese in the Indian Ocean in the sixteenth century all this changed. With the discovery of the Cape route there was now a viable alternative to trading through the Near East, and it was an Arab navigator, Ibn Majid, who showed the Portuguese how they could sail directly across the Indian Ocean by utilising the monsoon. This was the foundation of Portuguese fortunes in India and the Far East, which in turn directly stimulated the export market for Chinese porcelain, some of it even specifically designed for the Portuguese court. The Dutch in turn succeeded the Portuguese as the great trading nation in South-East Asia, and it is claimed that there are more Dutch forts and seventeenth-century buildings extant in Sri Lanka to this day than there are in Holland. Certainly many of the Dutch and Portuguese forts on the coast of India which we were to visit in the years to come produced much evidence of Chinese export ware, and in Quilon it was significant that besides the celadon, we also picked up a piece of Dutch faience.

Quilon was a puzzle, for surely a port of such importance should have left some trace. But we came to the conclusion that like many of the ports on the south-west coast of India, they were simply roadsteads, with the long-distance international shipping anchored out at sea, and the trade carried back and forth in smaller craft to the shore, which could more easily navigate the breakers. There were hundreds of such craft on the beach at Quilon. A couple of lads on the beach said there was an old port four kilometres to the north and tomorrow we could climb the lighthouse and survey the land. When we got back to the rest house it was dark and the lights were out. We had candles and an excellent curried chicken in a kitchen nearby, with the fruit we had bought, and tea, and gin. And there were still the mosquitos; we would see who won tomorrow.

In fact, we did; lots of insect repellent and repeated lighting of coils all night long kept them at bay, but it was still very hot and sticky. Kathy wasn't feeling at all well, and we went off to photograph from the headland by ourselves. Alas, we were forbidden to take the camera up the lighthouse (permission necessary from Madras), but the view from the top added little to that from below. There were miles of coconut groves, amongst which even the inland canals were invisible; and there was the curving beach to the south, with hundreds of little boats, many of them out fishing. To the north were a couple of rocky headlands similar to the one we were on, and there was nothing else. The lighthouse was built by the British in 1902, all brass and gleaming glass prisms, a beautiful machine.

On the way back we were pursued by hordes of children, tiresome as ever. I went down among the fishing boats to take some photographs looking south along the extraordinarily steep beach – the boats go in and out at an angle of almost 45°. It was an unsavoury walk, no flush toilets here. I met two Indian priests and asked them about the ancient port. They said it was always just like today, the little boats going out to meet the bigger ones at sea. This was later confirmed by the young clerk who changed my travellers' cheques in the bank in Quilon, who said they also on occasion built pontoons out to visiting ships. The trade itself was linked inland to a network of canals running for fifty miles north to Alleppey. The market in Quilon is tremendously active, and apart from all sorts of general merchandise, there was more fruit and vegetables of greater variety and quality and better displayed than anywhere else we had so far seen on our return trip through India. There were even gooseberries.

We collected Kathy and set off for Alleppey with our persistent click. It got worse and then the gearbox began to thump. I decided perhaps it wasn't the silencer after all, and drove Speedy up on to the verge and across two humps, so I could crawl below. At last the cause of all the noise was revealed; the rubberised bracket supporting the gearbox and shaft, in fact the whole rear end of the engine, was broken. We limped slowly along, fearful that we would have to get to Alleppey before we could get it fixed, another thirty kilometres away. But a mile or so along the road we came to a workshop by the wayside, busy making new cars out of a few old ones. Workers swarmed all over the car, and with their help I got the old bracket off. They then welded it together, and cut a new template to fit below as a reinforcement by using a sheet of metal and a cold chisel, even punching out two screw holes. They fixed it all back and asked for a rupee; I gave them ten.

We went straight on to Cochin, which turned out to be an awful muddle of a town, and by luck rather than judgement found our hotel, which was described in a guide as 'exotic'; it was plain dirty, but cheap, a bar and restaurant and a few faded rooms, and just about our standard these days. We thought to make up for it by eating in a 'good' restaurant in Ernakulam nearby; this took us an hour to find, and turned out to be another eatery/drinkery just like where we were staying. But we had a good and not too extortionate meal, and bumped back to the hotel.

Earlier in the day we had seen the northern part of Cochin, with mansions which would not have been out of place in Wimbledon, grouped round a football pitch, where cricket was in practice. Here also was the oldest church in India, AD 1503, the sometime resting place of Vasco da Gama. It was a barren hall with badly carved monuments now overlaid with Church of England taste. The most fascinating aspect was the hand-pulled fans, arranged E–W for the congregation and additionally above the pulpit and the lectern. We also found the Paradesi synagogue in the middle of Jew Town (thus inscribed on shop signs) but it was Saturday and the community at prayer.

On Sunday we had breakfast in the hotel and then went to see the synagogue. First we visited the old palace at Mattancherry next door, which was built by the Portuguese in 1557 for the Raja of Cochin, later extended by the Dutch. There was a Hindu temple on the ground floor, and another in the garden on the way to the synagogue. Upstairs in the palace, in airy rooms with shiny plastered floors were the remains of wall paintings, variously dated from the sixteenth century onwards. They were very complex to look at, almost if they were meant to be puzzles for people good at detecting oddities in the jungly landscape, like tigers and other animals. Some walls had traces of unfinished paintings sketched in an orange outline, which contrasted strangely with the complete paintings nearby which had an almost Stanley Spencer like precision. In the ladies' bedchamber the paintings were erotic, except the erotic acts were almost entirely confined to the animals in the distant landscape, who were copulating round every tree trunk. They were charmingly drawn, with the same graceful line as the unfinished paintings. Also in the palace were elegant palanquins with ivory inlay, a handsome table and a swing.

The synagogue was approached across a little playing field, up a narrow street from Jew Town. It was very spruce and well kept, and in the entrance paintings depicted the flight of the Jews to the east, and their subsequent history, ending up with Indira Gandhi's attendance at the 400th anniversary of the place of worship. The building was a simple structure with steps leading up to the Ark and a pulpit in the middle of the floor, which was dominated by rows of large Chinese blue-and-white tiles. The caretaker, Mr Jackie Cohen, took us around and showed us the copper deeds of AD 1000, giving special rights to the Jews, the collection of Torahs and a piece of inscribed skin. He told us about previous distinguished visitors, such as Lord Curzon who was given some of the Chinese tiles which are now in the British Museum; John Freeman, when he was High Commissioner; Lord Snowden, who promised to come back with his wife ('that was seven years ago'); and one of the Guinness ladies who was subsidising the preservation of Victorian India, who according to our guide when she was in Cochin was uninterested and rather rude. I was captivated by the tiles and whilst I was busy taking notes and photographs, groups of Indians came by, all of whom were given courteous treatment by Mr Cohen in his low-key way, and all of whom were rather rude too, with much giggling as if they were visiting the zoo. He was remarkably forebearing.

The tiles had been installed in 1762 by Ezekiel Rahabi during the refurbishment of the synagogue. There were 1,150 of them, of five different types, one slightly larger than the rest, painted either with Chinese landscapes or bouquets of peonies and other flowers, one with a willow tree. They are a minor footnote in the history of Chinese export porcelain, and I was to find out later that there were similar tiles in the collection of porcelain in Topkapi Sarayi in Istanbul, and in the Gayer Anderson Museum in Cairo. I have not been able to track down the one that Curzon gave to the British Museum, but I myself found another in Beirut. It turned out that Ezekiel Rahabi was a prominent merchant attached to the Dutch East India Company. The Dutch connection is intriguing, for it is known that Delft tiles were copied by the Chinese in porcelain, and these in turn exported to the Near East. As so often happened, the Chinese artists misunderstood the Dutch motif – a little thatched house on an island with a tree – and drew the house with the wall to the left of the tree missing. The Chinese tiles were in turn copied yet again by Armenian potters in Kütahya in Turkey in the early eighteenth century, who left out the house and tree entirely. Finally, there is a carpet in the Turkish and Islamic Museum in Istanbul where the central motif has clearly been lifted from the Dutch/Chinese tile, but the little house has now become the Ka'aba at Mecca.

By the time I was finished it was lunchtime, which this time was a fish curry in the hotel with all sorts of flavours in the rice, cardoman and cloves, raisins and other spices. It should be said that my initial reaction to south Indian curry was a fiery one, and it took some while before I could detect any flavour amongst the flames. I was also a convinced carnivore, and as the local cuisine was usually vegetarian, I was somewhat defeated. But the rest of the family was happy, and it is a matter of some surprise still considering what and where we ate that none of us came to serious grief. As Peggy maintained this was thanks to the Chlorox bottle; this had been recommended by a Lebanese doctor before we left, and a few drops put in the drinking water every day. I maintained that when we got back, and I had to have an x-ray for quite another matter, it revealed twenty-two feet of snow white intestines.

We turned inland from Cochin to the mountains, aiming for Ootacamund ('Snooty Ooty'), a hill station with a famous reputation in colonial times. We were defeated by endless road improvements as we climbed up from the coast, which slowed us down considerably. The scenery was attractive, with an open quality which was a relief from the claustrophobic coastal road, always too far inland to make one aware of the sea, and too much of a public highway to make driving a pleasure. We saw a whole flight of bright green parrots sitting on the telegraph wires, themselves supported on tall stone shafts. It was late afternoon, grey and cloudy over the mountains, with the sun lighting up different parts of the landscape in a very dramatic way, in fact very like the landscape in many Indian miniatures. Some of the rice paddies were already being harvested, and the village houses had steep gabled roofs and overhanging eaves. By the time we got to Coimbatore it was after dark, and too late for Snooty. The car also appeared to have snapped again below, so the first thing to do was to find a garage tomorrow. We found the rest house in the dark; as usual it was full, this time with policemen all in Coimbatore for 'Police Games', according to a banner we drove below. We ended up in the 'best' hotel, with a suite of irregular rooms including a triangular bathroom. There was some sort of celebration going on when we arrived, possibly the monthly meeting of the Coimbatore Lions Club. And in room 38, according to a tableful of testimonials and photos just outside the door, a well-known South Indian palmist was 'permanently camping'.

The garage turned out to be very efficient and the engineer in charge luckily once had a 1938 Morgan himself, so we skipped what would otherwise have been a four-week waiting list for repairs, and got to the top. But all the same it took another day as he did not have a spare foundation block and had to manufacture a new one. We were stuck at the hotel in our irregular suite, and according to the clerk Coimbatore is an industrial town with nothing to see besides a mechanical museum (?) and two inaccessible temples. So we spent all day washing clothes and writing letters, and I shopped for a bottle of gin. We also waited all day for a coherent reply from Mackinnon Mackenzie in Bombay, whom we telexed early in the morning, about the date of our departure. The agents were infuriating, unable to give a straight answer to a perfectly plain question; or perhaps they simply didn't know themselves. We had a lunch of vegetables and rice in the hotel, in the darkest restaurant I have ever been in, dark even for a shady nightclub past midnight.

We collected the car, now running very well indeed, and left for Ooty. First there was a series of hairpin bends climbing up through the ghats, but the road was very well designed and had the best surface we had been on for a long while. We travelled through jungle until the vegetation became progressively more alpine. When we finally got there, Ooty turned out to be rather awful, tea-planters' bungalows and clubs off a tatty main street, and a weedy racecourse, with much pretension. We ate lunch in a Chinese restaurant which might have been in the East End of London, even down to coloured views of Peking and the shiny scarlet paint. Continuing across a rolling green plateau, we descended the ghats on the other side, with some majestic scenery of greenery, rocks and waterfalls. We also passed three monkeys which were closer in size to apes, quite different to the Lanka monkeys we had become used to. Gradually the jungle grew sparser, and we arrived at Mysore just as night was falling, past an unbelievable Victorian palace with a strong flavour of the Mall all around. The town itself had a jumbled plan but a beautifully clean and attractive market on a slope, with fruit and vegetables in profusion and all sorts of other stalls on the periphery selling spices, nuts conical piles of coloured powder, deep red and purple. Everywhere incense sticks were burning so that the whole market smelled of a blend of sweetness and its own natural odours. One alley was entirely filled with baskets of different coloured flowers knotted into garlands. Peggy slipped back to buy two, for tomorrow was Kathy's seventeenth birthday.

We stayed in Mysore in a kind of Indian caravansarai, all of the rooms on three storeys with continuous balconies opening on to a central courtyard with a little cafe-restaurant. We visited the Art Museum, a redundant palace with miles of bad painting, awful furniture and knick knacks. There was nothing even funny to laugh at, just an unending quantity of dreadful objects. Thoroughly depressed we returned to the hotel to load up, and we had just got out of town when the dip switch/horn/direction indicator snapped off the steering column. We found a garage, and after an unsuccessful attempt to solder the broken elements, I got them to replace the broken arm with a screwdriver sharpened and rammed into the socket, and the horn reconnected to a spare switch. This took time, and it was one o'clock before we set off again.

Just as we turned on to the main road from the garage, we met a strange procession coming towards us. A cheerful crowd was carrying aloft an elderly and very dead man, dressed in a business suit and sitting on a shoulder-high armchair. His face was both dark and ashen at the same time, the lower part wound with a scarf presumably to keep his jaw up. The mourners all carried little yellow chrysanthemums in bunches and garlands. There was music of some kind, and the whole procession was breathtakingly bizarre. When we mentioned seeing the dead man to Andy, he categorically refused to accept it *was* a dead man and was quite convinced it was a dummy.

After an unsuccessful attempt to see the fort at Srirangapatnam – we were all too tired to work up any enthusiasm – we set off on what we thought was the road to Shravan Belgola. An hour later we realised we had curved round and were on our way westwards to Mangalore. We got back on the road north to Hassan, and then swung off to the right across sixteen miles of deserted countryside, rather like moorland, to the foot of the hill on which the statue of Shravan Belgola stands, perhaps the greatest of all Jain monuments. It was evening, and leaving Speedy behind we climbed up the stairs cut in the great rock in our bare feet, the stone still warm from the day's sun. From the top you look down on the town below, rather like a reconstruction of a Roman town, with a regular plan and tiled red roofs around a great central tank full of olive-green water. Behind the town is a further jumble of boulders and hills, slightly lower, with more temples on top.

We climbed on upwards, through a gate in a circumference wall, across more boulders and past a temple propped up long ago with inclined stone slabs, up another staircase and to the left and right through more gates until we at last reached the main entrance. Through the doorway into the central courtyard, the first thing you see are two gigantic toes, covered with flowers and other offerings. As you advance into the courtyard, the gigantic figure rises above you, smoothly and cleanly carved out of the mountain like some oriental *kourai*. The feet are planted in a rock carved with strange orifices, with the beginnings and ends of snakes, and rivulets for liquid offerings, all set in a ring of carved lotus petals. The legs swell up to a great stone penis, uncircumcised, with the foreskin neatly spiralled, hanging limp but firm and swollen with life. Above, the torso has massive wide shoulders and the head is carved with great precision. The arms are garlanded with leaves. From the top of the temple walls you can admire the tightly designed curls of the god's hair, and his neat, rounded bottom.

Quite apart from the central image, the whole temple complex is ingeniously designed and the total effect not unlike the Parthenon, with its interrelation of separate temple units. No one seemed to mind my taking photographs, but ruefully I ran out of film and I didn't fancy running down five hundred steps to the car for more. The detailed carving included animals and fishes in low relief, and footprints and elephants and other animals traced in the rock beside the staircase. The moment I was leaving, I saw a rat run quickly to the foot of the statue and snatch a garland of yellow dahlias from the big toe, running off with it trailing behind him.

We reluctantly descended and drove a further fifteen miles in the dark, to the Indian Government rest house at Hassan. Here we had an altercation, for after agreeing to the price for a double room, the clerk was replaced by the night clerk, who told us we had to pay for three beds. So we made him change us to a three-bed room, which meant much moving of luggage and frayed tempers. I went out in the dark and bought a rupee's worth of dirty peanuts from a pressure-lit stand by the roadside, and with some apples and bananas we had a picnic in our triple room and decided to make an early start the next day. But I still could not get over that extraordinary Jain statue. After the reclining Buddha at Polonnaruwa, it was the most impressive piece of sculpture we had seen. Carved about the year AD 1000, for a thousand years it had been an active place for Jain pilgrimage. Nowadays, we were told, at the major festival every few years, he is anointed from above with offerings poured from a hovering helicopter.

The local guidebook succinctly sums up the experience:

> As we pass through the main gate our eyes are captivated by Sri Gommateswara Swamy, and we stand speechless, wanderstruck at hisunequalled byanty.
>
> SRAVANABELGOLA
> A Colour Publication
> Tourist Concern, Mysore.

9

THE CRASH

By now the journey back home through India had assumed a rhythm all of its own. Any serious hunting for sherds was over, for by now we were travelling inland away from the coast. Still without precise information about when our boat would leave Bombay, we drove north at a fair speed, with a little sightseeing to liven things up on our way. There is a certain repetitiveness in my diary for this period; each day presented the same problems to be solved in the same sequence. Getting up, paying the bill, getting loaded and getting off. Then the search for something to eat and somewhere reasonably modest to stay. And making sure Speedy performed properly was an extra anxiety, for an alarming number of parts seemed to fall off, as a result of the bumpy roads and the fact that we were distinctly overloaded. Apart from the four of us and our general luggage, we had acquired a very heavy Maldivian teak chess board from Male, a model boat, thirteen pieces of Persian pottery, a Maldivian native dress and silver chain, a celadon stem cup and an enamelled Swatow bowl, quite apart from several hundred potsherds which weighed extremely heavy. And cooped up in the car there were inevitably squabbles, which evaporated almost as soon as they blew up, often about the most trivial matters. Peggy acted as moderator and cheerfully kept the lid on most of the time. Kathy was already mentally back in Beirut and at school again with all her friends. And Andy was free at last, to scamper around when the occasion presented itself; he had his plaster cast sawn off in Colombo by a very elderly and wobbly doctor, with an enormous circular saw. The slightest slip and Andy's fragile arm would have come off too, and any moment I expected a fountain of blood. In short, we all felt that the excitement of the trip was over, and all we had to do was to get home safe and sound. Also, psychologically there was a big difference for me between Ceylon and India. Ceylon seemed so remote, cast out in the Indian Ocean, that one always had the feeling that it was hardly of this world, whereas in India one had the sense of the familiar, of being on a continent rather than an island. It is difficult to pin this down precisely, but on this and subsequent visits to Ceylon I have always left with relief, almost congratulating myself on having made it out alive.

After Shravan Belgola, we went to visit two more temples, this time Hindu ones, at Halebid and Belur. The first, Halebid, was the epitome of what I had always imagined an Indian temple to look like, perhaps because it has been reproduced so many times. Carved out of weathered grey stone, it is symmetrical in plan and covered with layer upon layer of ornament on the outside, friezes of elephants, chariots, dancers, wagons and warriors all quite small in scale and in the greatest detail. Inside turned pillars support a complex post-and-lintel structure where the basic design is lost amongst the profusion of decoration. All together, we agreed, it was too much of a good thing, and had none of the drama of the great Jain statue yesterday. We continued on to Belur, which is of approximately the same date and in the same idiom, and had a similar reaction to it. We did not linger long.

We drove on through the village of Chickmagalur, on our way to Jog Falls, where we hoped to spend the night. Just short of another village called Tarikere, we were behind a

THE CRASH

dusty red bus. It was about nine o'clock in the morning, and we were both travelling not more than 30 mph. I sounded the horn twice, and saw the conductor turn round to look at us. The bus suddenly stopped dead in the middle of the road, I slammed on the brakes, and we rammed straight into the back of it.

Silence.

We realised we were all conscious, but the dashboard was smashed, the windscreen in a million pieces and the steering wheel crumpled on my chest. I felt all right; Peggy was white as a sheet and beginning to bleed profusely. Kathy was in a daze, having been asleep when the crash came; she was badly hit on her forehead and the top of her head. Andy was completely unhurt and quite calm. The doors were jammed, and we all got out across my door, which didn't have the side windows on. The driver and his few passengers got out of the bus and came back to see what had happened.

I sat Peggy down on the roots of a tree on the roadside, for she was streaming with blood. I washed her head as best as possible, and found a deep gash on the back of her head, and her face was badly cut; she complained of glass in her mouth, and a painful knee. It was obvious that the first thing to do was to get Peggy's wounds dressed properly, but first we had to unload the car of all its luggage and get it and us onto the bus. For the first time I appreciated what a wreck the car was. The chassis under the engine was buckled back on either side and the whole of the front smashed into the engine. The back was relatively intact. In fact we were remarkably lucky to be alive, a fact which we quickly consoled ourselves with in our shock at such a speedy end to Speedy, and our journey. The only thing to do was to try to put some sort of a pattern onto the chaos with which we had so suddenly been presented. We went in the bus, first to the tiny rest house in Tarikere to set down the baggage and the children, then to the 'hospital' across the street – in reality a birth-control clinic – conveniently next to the police station.

No one was around in the clinic, as it was lunchtime by now, and a glimpse inside revealed a deeply stained wooden board with a tiny blotched dark pillow at one end. Filthy sinks and bowls, and old dressings on the floor completed the forlorn ensemble. It looked like a parody of a back-street abortionist's parlour. At last a nursing sister came, and she sent for the doctor, who was having his lunch. A crowd of curious villagers were at the door, some even climbing in the window. The doctor shooed them away and began to berate his staff for not having called him sooner. I tried to draw his attention to the patient, for Peggy was covered with coagulating blood, running down her neck and all over her clothes. I took the cloth off the table in the next room, and we proceeded with a wound-by-wound inspection. Her nose, chin and forehead all had glass cuts, and her knee was also bleeding, but worst of all was the long gash right to the skull on the back of her head. The doctor nervously told the sister to put a stitch in it, obviously having no intention of doing it himself.

She threaded an enormous needle with double strands of what looked like homespun cotton, and lifting up a piece of flesh jabbed it through. Poor Peggy, who thankfully could not see what was happening, thought this was all, and winced when the whole performance was repeated on the other side, the simplest of knots being tied to bring the scalp together. A lot of hair was cut off and a large dressing applied, with smaller ones for the other wounds, everyone having a good fingering of the dressings first.

The doctor had coffee brought to us and we retired very shaken to the rest house. Later, after lunching on a curious herbal omelette, a policeman came. He was the first of many visitors, including an official from the bus company, nervous that I should lodge a complaint, and the head of the Rotary Club in the village, solicitous that foreigners should have come to grief in their midst. We had a hot dinner of peppery rice, mutton and chicken curry, and went mournfully to bed, full of woe, Peggy in great discomfort, Kathy with a splitting headache, Andy tired and nervous and myself with an aching chest, with which I had broken the steering wheel. In the night mosquitoes zoomed in to add to our misery.

Morning eventually came and we had a visit from another policeman, from the next village, Lingavallah, ten miles away on the other side of the crash. I had been told last night that I had to go there and report to its police station, as it was within that parish that the accident had occurred. I was put on the 6am bus, but at the end of the village street I abandoned ship, realising the folly of going off at that early hour, and almost certainly not being able to get back again. I went to *our* police station, and was much helped by a visiting sanitary inspector, who explained the finer points to the other officers in the room, who were all sitting like myself at high, sloping tables like Dickensian clerks. To have it done with, I copied out the statement I had carefully prepared on an official form, but the local officer would not witness it and said he would pass it on to Lingavallah.

Things then took a less gracious turn. A policeman arrived from Lingavallah and said he was waiting for the doctor's report, and then we would go together to Lingavallah Police Station. He began to shout, and said it was all my fault for not stopping – I was speeding, and my brakes didn't work, and he was determined I should be arrested as the criminal party. He left me to wait for him.

I waited from midday until after two, and had a brief encounter with officials from the bus company, a new one and the nervous one who came last night. I went to see the doctor, who was also lodging in the rest house, and he was in the middle of his report. He had also been visited by the ferocious shouter, and had the same impression that the blame was to be laid at my door. He told me that the case must come before the Magistrate, hopefully tomorrow, and that I should describe my version of events, and even if possible see the Magistrate this evening, when he came to the doctor to have his blood pressure checked! A policeman friend of the doctor's said I should also see the Circle Inspector in our police station, who had authority over the Sub-Inspector at Lingavallah, and that there would be difficulties at Lingavallah, because I would have to be formally charged, and they could not release me except on surety of someone in India, which of course we did not have.

I began to see the picture a little clearer, and set off for Lingavallah on the 3pm bus, quite prepared to spend the night there. Peggy was distraught. The policeman and myself sat in the front seat behind the driver, whom I noted had only one side mirror, and who also stopped firmly in the middle of the road all the way. I pleaded with my stern policeman to stop for one minute at the wreck, which he reluctantly agreed to, and then regretted when I whipped out my camera and quickly took pictures of the wreck. He was exhorting me to get back in the bus, when the young curly-headed policeman who was on guard at the wreck insisted on having his photograph taken too. I suggested tomorrow, but he plaintively said that he wouldn't be on duty tomorrow. So I did.

The police station in Lingavallah was even more of a village affair, with a garden in front and offices behind, and we waited for the Sub-Inspector, who had to be fetched from his home across the cow-patch. He had a large moustache and was equally fierce, starting off in a very belligerent manner, saying I must stay and no authority could overrule his. Then two voices chimed in from behind; it was the two bus company officials, and the picture became clearer still. The pressure was being put on, and the reward of release would be paid for by perjury. The driver of the bus had lodged a complaint against me after the accident for careless driving, and it was I who was on trial. My defence could only be made when the case was heard, and my testimony was unacceptable. I was a careless driver, going too fast. I pointed out I had just come from Rameswaram, and asked how long this would take? 'Two days', they said. I replied I had taken eight. My brakes were obviously at fault, they said, as I had not stopped. I grabbed my bag and produced my trump card, my bill from Stones Garage of two days ago, evidence that the car was in full working condition. Consternation. I demanded in turn to know why the bus rear lights had not worked when it stopped. 'They did', said the new bus company man, and to *my* consternation produced a certificate and waved it under the Sub-Inspector's nose, to certify that he had personally inspected the bus's lights on 28 August and had signed to that effect.

Now the conversation took a serious turn, with the bus company man taking over from the Sub-Inspector. *If* I pleaded guilty before the Magistrate, a little fine, 50 rupees, perhaps 100 rupees ('25', interrupted the Sub-Inspector) and everything would be finished, he would bring a mechanic, transport my wife and family to Shimoga, have the Basheer Garage work on repairing the car, and we could depart on time. *If not*, if I made complications and defended myself, how long might the case go on? I might have to stay one, two, three more days, miss the boat ...

By this time the Sub-Inspector had withdrawn from the argument, and it was between me and the bus company. The Vehicle Inspector from Chickmagalur, who should have come to inspect the wreck this afternoon, never arrived. Until his report arrives, the Magistrate cannot try the case. But I cannot stay, I said; I will give you my passport as bail, and I have an appointment to see the Magistrate at 6pm. Collapse of the Sub-Inspector, and I was allowed to go back to Tarikere on the 4.15pm bus, and I would see the Magistrate, and they would do everything to make the case go as quickly as possible, otherwise it may be four days, five days ...

I caught the bus back and waved to the policeman at the wreck, and left the bus at the beginning of Tarikere, as a quantity of passengers wanted to get on. It is 'holiday' in Tarikere, market day, and I passed a great open market with fruit and flowers on display and many oddments cooking in batter at stalls including green peppers, the equivalent of fish and chips I suppose.

Back in the bosom of my relieved family, I told all about the day's events. Later, seven men knocked at the door, with the two bus men in front, full of assurances that tomorrow the car will be saved and all will be well, and on Sunday we will go to Jog Falls whilst the car is repaired, and on Monday we will be on our way again to Bombay. After all, said the first bus man, you are foreigners and everyone feels sorry for you, and it is my duty to do for you what you would do for me in your country. Apparently even perjury, if necessary. As Peggy observed last night, it takes a crisis to make one realise how unimportant are many of the things one worries about.

We went uncomfortably to bed, only to be startled awake at about half past one in the morning. Someone was carefully trying to open the door. Silence. Then a few minutes later someone tried to force the second door into the room, from inside the rest house. Silence again. There were lights outside, and distant muttering. Again, the doors were tried; I checked that they were all securely bolted on the inside. We decided to keep all the lights off and make no noise. A few minutes later there was a loud banging on the door and rattling of the lock – but no voice. It could not have been the police, else they would have identified themselves. It was certainly whoever had first tried to get into the room surreptitiously. I put the Chlorox and a tumbler on the table, the only weapon I could think of, ready to dash in the eyes of the intruder if he succeeded in breaking down the door. After checking the locks again – there were four doors leading into the room – and the windows, we went back to an uneasy sleep, wondering if we would wake up in time to defend ourselves if the intruder burst in.

We were woken about quarter to six by the sound of birds chirping outside the window, and went back to sleep again until it was fully light. Last night was a thoroughly alarming experience, and we speculated on whom it could possibly have been. Perhaps the bus driver had sent a few friends to coerce us, for he had the most to lose if I argued against him in court. Or perhaps it had been a common thief. Or maybe someone after Kathy's virginity. But Kathy had suffered from victims of another sort – bed bugs. Her neck and her body were covered all over with swollen lumps, and we chased a couple of them across the dirty counterpane.

At about 9.30am the policeman from Langavallah arrived, to tell us the Traffic Inspector had never arrived, so they had come with all the evidence so far to present to the Magistrate. Would we please be at the Court at 10.30. He was uneasy in the presence of the family, much less aggressive than he had been in his own office, and said he wanted the whole case finished as quickly as possible. We also met the doctor, who advised me whatever I did not to plead not guilty. For if I did, there would have to be a proper trial, and such was the waiting list in India it might take up to six months before the case was heard.

We went to the court, a single-storey building with a long room with tables all round and a raised platform at one end. I was sat on the defendant's bench in the open courtyard. About half an hour later, a thin and shaky figure wearing a Nehru cap passed by with an umbrella, heading for a room opposite marked BAR ASSOCIATION; this must surely be the high pressure Magistrate. Then the President of the Rotary Club, a lawyer, came by and asked us what had happened. We told him, and he said he would look after us and find out what was happening. In the meanwhile he installed us in the outer chamber of the BAR ASSOCIATION, in wicker chairs, to stare at group photos of past magistrates, and wait whilst self-assured young lawyers whizzed in and out, most of them (like the Magistrate) on the way to the all-evident lavatory on our immediate left. Our lawyer returned, to tell us the traffic report still had not yet arrived, and the formal charge of negligence not yet put to the court; would we please come back again at one o'clock. Then hopefully, if I pleaded guilty, the case might even be disposed of without the elusive report on Speedy's imperfections. I reflected I could write a better one, like a lover recording his mistresses' blemishes; alas, everyone else would only recognise her as That Woman ... We retired to the rest house to wait, and I chased a pack of naughty girls climbing in the windows. I caught one by the arm, and she burst into tears; games are not supposed to end with victims. I gave her one of my crossest looks and let her go; she ran quickly away and it appeared to do the trick momentarily, for the landscape was now clear of kids. There was no sign either of the motor men or the promised Basheer from his garage in Shimoga. We worried if the Magistrate might pass out before lunchtime, he certainly looked seedy enough. The court sat until five, as there were plenty of other cases to be heard. Nobody knew when it would convene again.

We got back to the court and everything had been arranged, the police becoming a little more friendly. Through the open window I heard all the documents being examined and discussed. Then I was led into the courtroom and made to stand between the tables, facing the judge. He read the accusation. 'Are you Guilty or Not Guilty?' of rushing into the bus; 'Guilty, Your Honour, but with extenuating circumstances'. I added that I may well have been guilty of negligence but this was compounded by a mechanical failure in the car. The Magistrate, who turns out *not* to be the failing aged party but a much younger, sprucer man, lent forward and asked if I would like to give written or oral evidence. I opted for the latter, and gave a varnished account of events ending with thanks to the driver, passengers, doctor and nurse for all their help after the accident. This turned out to be ironic, as it now seemed that five peasants (euphemistically termed 'agriculturalists') had turned in evidence against me in Hindi, copies of which are presented to me by the Magistrate. The Magistrate wrote at some length in his ledger, then turns to me with obvious pleasure, exonerated me from crime and fined me 20 Rupees for my negligence. There are smiles all round, and I suddenly become *persona grata* with everyone, who are all so pleased that I pleaded guilty that I seemed to have automatically joined some sort of exclusive club. I paid the fine and now the wreck could be released. We proceeded into cars to the scene of the accident. But first there was a long altercation amongst the bus company men. I enquired what the problem was. The answer was, who was going to pay for the damage to the bus? At this I exploded, and told them that everyone from the Magistrate downwards knew full well it was the driver's fault and that I only pleaded guilty for a quick release. If they dared mention money, they could try the insurance company, but I would certainly tell Head Office in Bombay precisely what happened. No more was heard of this.

When we approached the wreck I noticed the policeman guarding it had thrown his jacket over the top. He slunk off, and after he had departed I discovered the jacket had been hiding an enormous hole in the top of the car; he must have slept in it with his oil lamp, which had set fire to the roof. The officer from Langavallah shrugged his shoulders. Then Basheer, who had arrived with the bus company men after the trial, proceeded to pull the car apart. It was obvious it was beyond repair in India. The chassis was distorted and the front completely smashed in. But the wheels were free and the car could just be steered. I stripped it of every detachable piece and we towed it back to Tarikere, where we parked it behind the rest house to the joy of hundreds of children.

We were cheered up by a visit from the lawyer of the Rotary Club, who said he would do everything he could to help us, and so truly meant it he provided a sharp contrast with the other rogues. First, Basheer began with a demand for 250 Rupees for the afternoon's work. He settled for 100. As 150 had disappeared from my trousers' pocket at the wreck that afternoon when I was dismantling the car, and he had also siphoned off 100 Rupees of petrol now, alas, no longer needed for my tank, he didn't do too badly. The lawyer suggested we discuss means of moving the wreck, whether by train or sending it by truck to Bombay. We couldn't leave it behind, because then we would have technically imported it, and although a complete wreck we would be obliged to pay something like eight times its new value as import tax. We settled for a truck although it would probably cost 1,200–1,500 Rupees. The lawyer also had us moved for the night from our filthy room to the front of the rest house, which was spotlessly clean by comparison and relatively mosquito proof.

After dark, the doctor arrived and was very pleased when we told him the positive result of taking his good advice. 'Well done, old chap, now you can bugger off!', he kept repeating. The Magistrate had already told him of my guilty plea. I gave him some of our spare drugs for use in the hospital, and this pleased him too. We asked him if there was anything we could do about Kathy's bites. He broke into a wide grin and said, 'It's bugs, man, bugs!'. A little later when we were enveloped in our ghostly mosquito nets he knocked on the door, to invite us to another room for 'some drinks'. But it was too late, and much though we could have used one by this stage we demurred.

We woke early and scuttled back to our old room, having promised to abandon the better one by 7am, as a visitor of importance was expected. I started to strip more off the car, and about 9.30am the lawyer arrived to take us for breakfast in his little two-storey house just a few yards away. He had a pretty wife, two sons and a daughter, and we had metal plates of nuts, coconut fudge and an apple, and crispy fried bananas, biscuits and milky coffee. It was all very good.

He told us about himself. His father had died when he was two, and he had two sisters. His mother had to manage the family land in a village about ten miles away by herself; they were going on their weekly visit today. He had gone to school in Bangalore, where one of his sisters had married. Her husband had taken a fancy to him, and thanks to his patronage he had become a lawyer. He didn't want to become a magistrate, as he felt he would lose his independence by becoming a government official. He truly believed he could do more by working directly as a lawyer with the people and described himself as a sort of social psychiatrist. Unbelievably, there were nineteen lawyers in Tarikere, and the court sat six

THE CRASH

days a week. This seemed to suggest an abnormal love of litigation in the area. He was a very genuine fellow (or chap, as one would say in Tarikere), and it was sad to hear him on the subject of the lack of incentive for the Indian middle classes, and the future of the country with all its complex problems. We took leave of him after taking photographs of each of our families on the roof of his house, and we parted with all our luggage for Shimoga thirty miles away, to look for a lorry. We left the wreck of Speedy under a tarpaulin.

At Shimoga we had to walk half a mile to the guest house, which we later found out had been built by the grandfather of a coffee planter as a circuit house in imperial days. One could still see the effect he was aiming at. The rounded, projecting entrance with rows of twin columns, the entrance hall with empty niches, the trees close by framing a distant view of fields and cattle (and now, factories), the shrubbery, potted plants and wickerwork chairs, all combined to create the illusion of a Nash pavilion accidentally set down in India. Inside it was grubby, but a distinct improvement on the rest house in Tarikere.

We telephoned our next Rotary contact, another lawyer, and he came quickly and took charge of the situation. He found us a lorry, and checked with his brother who owned a steel mill that often sent material to Poona that the price was right. The price was right all right, but astronomical for our meagre budget – 2,800 Rupees, about £150, more than double the estimate in Tarikere, and twice the cost of shipping the car from Bombay to Kuwait. We did some anxious sums, and decided we were stuck; there was no way round it. We would have to deal with the resulting insolvency when we returned to Beirut. However, we got the truck owner to agree that we should all be transported with our baggage as well, and deposited in Bombay at the quay side for the boat.

We returned to Tarikere for Speedy. It was now dark. We had been delayed as the truck had knocked down two telegraph poles on setting out and the driver first had to pay a visit to the police. Loading the car on to the lorry was finally accomplished by lifting it bodily four feet and sliding it in from the back. It was now moonlight. When we finally arrived back in Shimoga it was too late to start our long journey northwards, so we retired once again to the guest house.

10

BOMBAY AND BACK

I ROSE AT SIX next morning, to find I seemed to be all alone in the Nash pile. Most of the doors were locked, and there were no servants in the kitchen. Outside there was dew on the grass. There was no water either, and when the cook finally appeared, he went down to the end of the field and did something with a large spanner, which seemed to do the trick.

The truck came, and also its owner on a scooter. It was all agreed; money in advance, our passage to the ship with the car assured, and the driver and crew to stay on an extra day if necessary, remembering the time it had taken to get the car into India on our arrival. The driver was unshaven, looking rather like a Delacroix sketch. He had big bare feet, khaki shirt and shorts, and jumped around a lot and drove very fast. At the first opportunity after we set off he lit a bunch of incense sticks, and when they were quietly smoking touched the plastic image above the windscreen with them, then the dashboard and himself (but not us), and various gods to the right and behind our heads. We were sitting four in a row on a narrow seat across the cab behind him. I could not make out the images, five plastic figures in a row painted with shiny colours and lustrous gold, in a glass box. The one in front had a red light constantly pulsating before it. We had bought a pretty garland of white flowers and chrysanthemum heads before we left, and these were hung up along with strings of yellow flowers that the driver had purchased. It was all very gay, and we bounced along with everything jiggling from right to left, ourselves included. I found I could only read by using a strip of paper and moving it down the page line by line.

The countryside was pleasantly green and undulating but not particularly interesting. Soon we reached the main road to Bangalore, and began to travel the route we had taken two months ago in reverse. We stopped for food and drink in truckers' cafes which we had never noticed before, rather like café routières in France. They were very good and we had a delicious lunch in a dark cavern, produced from an even darker hole at the back. In front of all the cafes a sign popped out at lunchtime saying MEALS READY, as if lots of hungry eaters were waiting in the streets for the word.

It confirmed once again that the accident had brought into sharp focus something that we might never have experienced about India otherwise. Simply, the nasty turned incredibly nasty, like vultures waiting to feed on the corpse of our misfortune; and the nice so generous and helpful that it made it almost impossible to register any criticism at all. There did not seem to be any grey area in between, except perhaps the myriads of children who avidly followed every development in our small drama; and to give them the benefit of the doubt, there was no malice in their curiosity, although they were a little too nosey for my taste. The accident had become a sort of open-air theatre, in which we were the unwilling players. Never did I feel it more strongly than the moment after the impact. All those peasants surrounding the car, watching Peggy sitting bleeding on a tree stump, and myself and the children frantically trying to get the luggage out of the shattered car. All of us were somehow part of a drama which touched their real lives at no point at all.

Disembarrassed of the car at last, but not of the paper complications which were to last several days more, we found that our ship, the *Dwarka*, had had its departure postponed yet again. This left us with almost a week with nothing to do in Bombay. We considered going to Hyderabad, where there was reputedly a collection of Chinese porcelain in the museum, but at that moment it all seemed too complicated and exhausting, and potentially expensive. And we had also found the perfect niche for us in Bombay, the Y.W.C.A.

This was a small block of new, bright rooms overlooking a triangular playing field, surrounded by houses of the Edwardian period, many of which had been converted into schools. It was in the centre of town, and our balcony on the second floor looked straight into a magnolia tree, permanently infested with crows who had designs on our breakfast. Once, when I was lying in bed, listening to their sinister cawing, I wondered if they had designs on us, too. Below, each day a succession of children of both sexes trooped out to the playground to line up, march, do exercises and be harangued by their teachers. In the evening, lesser boys would come to play football, and the grass was worn bare in large patches by all this cheerful activity. The houses round about had wooden balconies and the scene completed by erratic palm trees towering above more deciduous varieties. All the young men and women employed as staff by the Y.W.C.A. were so friendly, and the hostel so bright and clean, that it was hard to imagine what more could be offered by the most expensive hotel. I returned to the Kafkaesque customs, and after three misdirections we found ourselves at the office of the customs officer who had previously let me examine the car myself, as it had been raining too hard for him and his scooter. With a tolerant gesture he outlined the steps I would have to climb; it was indeed only an outline, for each step turned out to have several intermediary steps, which he kept quiet about. With the lorry still parked outside the shipping agent's office, we scurried around from office to office with a fast growing sheaf of forms. Even within the offices, no one seemed to know which desk we should be at, and inevitably when we found the right location it was only to learn that a previous step had not been properly completed. Most of the officials were as kind as could be, mainly because of the gaunt spectre of a bandaged woman. When Peggy said she had a headache, aspirins were immediately produced; apparently every clerk takes one to the office each day just in case. The whole process had its own slow rhythm of signature and countersignature. But to move from one level to the next – literally, as every next desk seemed to be on the third floor of yet another liftless building – made one painfully aware of the very fragile connection between the parts, and the lack of any strong controlling hand. The system seemed designed to ensure nobody cheats anybody else, personally or departmentally, and to employ the maximum amount of persons for the minimum amount of time. I suppose it is one way of soaking up a surplus of literate middle-class men, a kind of government subsidy to reward the fruits of education.

The nicest of all were the workers permanently stationed on the quayside, the shed supervisor and his staff. I had met them all when we had first come to Bombay, and it was like a reunion of old friends. They were all very alarmed to hear about the accident and sad to see the car. These were of course the men who actually did the work of loading and unloading, as opposed to the abstraction of the paper bureaucrats. Their work seemed more real and their relationships with each other more human, because the situation demanded a kind of cooperation unnecessary in an office from desk to desk. Although probably less well paid, there was an air of easy camaraderie amongst them. The supervisor, far from being tough, was a quiet, shy man who gave most of his orders with a nod of his head.

The road had seemed endless and I recognised little of our previous drive except the general feeling of the landscape. Gradually night came, as we tossed about on the uneven bench; we tried every conceivable position, only to become aware that the most comfortable of all was sitting bolt upright.

The night was agonising, only relieved by another meal, and about six o'clock in the morning we found ourselves in the misty hills near Poona, where we stopped beside a stream to wash. After evading a tax station on the road, which wanted to claim 10 per cent of the value of the car for the Bombay municipality, we finally rolled into the city. What a contrast to our first encounter; coming in from the countryside, we were overwhelmed by its sophistication and signs of civilisation. It all seemed so clean now, but then we could hardly have been more scruffy and bedraggled.

We stopped at the doors of Mackinnon Mackenzie, the shipping agents. It was 10.30 and in usual Bombay business style the office was almost empty. I eventually found the head of the shipping department, a heavily built Anglo-Indian with impeccable English and a most disinterested reaction to our plight. I told him I wanted to deposit the car as quickly as possible near the quay from which it would be shipped. He suggested that as they were only responsible for the boat, I must find a shipping agent. It was not until a second visit and I embarrassed him by planting a bandaged wife at the edge of his desk that he uneasily put down a sheaf of telexes he was shuffling, and began to give us some advice. I realised I was going to have to repeat the whole import process, but in reverse. I asked him to tell the drivers, which he did in fluent Hindi, that they must stay another day if necessary. My Delacroix sketch turned nasty, lied and said this had never been agreed, and this would be another 150 Rupees. I was surprisingly adamant considering he had been told twice to the contrary in Shimoga, but then Shimoga was now four hundred miles away. I could have cheerfully put him on a Parsee tower for vulturising at that moment. He had already during the trip used the remaining space on the back of the lorry as an informal bus, and whenever we stopped I found the remains of Speedy packed around tight with wide-eyed faces clutching shapeless bundles. Two youths even survived as far as Bombay, to be put out on the busy streets.

Peggy's wound steadily healed, and one day we called a lady doctor to snip out the stitch. A professional woman, Indian style, she was more concerned that we had missed seeing Goa, where her family was from, than with the stitch. She had an attractive matter-of-fact manner, and after a polite farewell swept off with her black bag tucked under her arm to her next operation elsewhere. We all still ached from time to time; the impact of the crash had lasted longer than we had anticipated. But quiet days spent in Bombay were exactly what we all needed.

First of all, Bombay is a real town, in a sense that Beirut is not. There are wide streets and an even wider variety of buildings, the fixed points provided by the railway station, the Prince of Wales Museum, the post office, the port, the new hotels and a Manhattan-like complex of modern buildings on the southern tip. The mass of people everywhere is overwhelming, and adding to the general animation were the pavement parasites, some offering up spectacles like *no* arms, *no* legs, others clutching infants, and hundreds of children all imploring. Even to deal with one in ten is a task, but one's heart goes out not so much to the energetic supplicants but rather those who have given up and who lie in a dazed sleep in the middle of the pavement.

The attraction of city life is so obvious; it *is* richer, more varied and interesting in its possibilities, and more rewarding potentially than the inexorable and never-changing pattern of village life. The injection process from country to city life is painful, and many thousands must never make a successful transition. Those that do must move through many strata of society, which even a casual visitor can identify by the buildings in which people dwell, from the street upwards.

The part of Bombay where we were, near the museum, dated mostly from the late nineteenth century and up to the twenties. The west side of the park leading up to the neo-Gothic splendour of Churchgate Railway Station must have been developed during the thirties, with a profusion of rounded balconies, windows like portholes and decorative ironwork. The names of the apartment buildings almost always included the word COURT, and SUNSHINE COURT, a sprightly essay in thirties idiom, was next door to MOONLIGHT COURT, where the style was appropriately quieter and more subdued. Round the corner was REVIERA COURT. Years later I discovered from Hugh Casson, who also had a passion for Bombay buildings, that some of the many European architects who fled from Germany before the war ended up in India, which explained the modernist style. The light at that time of year was soft, but had great clarity. One morning walking to the post office the street looked like something out of a Canaletto, and some of the buildings were even in a sub-Venetian style with fading pinks and yellows, above them floating puffy white clouds against a typically Canaletto grey-blue sky fading quickly towards the horizon.

A week was long enough to try a variety of different restaurants in the city and they contrasted strangely with each other. An early find was Gordon's, part of a well-known chain with branches abroad. This was on the ground floor of a building looking out on Sir Narriman Road, close to Churchgate. Here again the decoration was in thirties style, with some interesting furniture of that period. There was a long sideboard and a serving table, emerald green and shiny black, with strongly sculptural forms. The tables were plain and the napkins coarse, and the menu was European and not especially good. The general feeling was like a lesser Groppi's in Cairo. It was the evening of our arrival, and the children found the consoling European ambience just right, and given half the chance I think they would have returned there for the rest of our stay. The following night we went to the Bristol Grill, Kathy in pursuit of its reputation for the best vegetarian food in town, and myself speculating on the carnivorous pleasures implicit in its name. But she was right, and I was wrong, and once again we were back to *puri* and curried vegetables, but that was all. The tables, both rectangular and circular, had tops stepped up in diminishing layers with slabs of glass on top. The banquettes had arm rests projecting like seaside piers, with eyeless, dimmed beacons set in their ends. Here the prevailing colours were shiny black and scarlet.

We also tried a cafe at the end of the road, somewhat typical of all the large, noisy cafes all the way down the street. The food was indifferent, perhaps because we were too late; the children said they had better luck there another day. But the customers made up for it. Along one wall, half a dozen flappers attracted the Bombay equivalent of the opposite sex; at another table, two young men and a girl, obviously the sister of one, devoured a pile of revolting cakes, all different colours like cassata, smothered in cream of Brylcream quality. They held each one at finger's length, poised, to regard it before casting down the hatch. The boys then lit up cigarettes, looking very white against their faces, and also held them aloft for inspection before inhaling.

But our great discovery, which we had tried and failed to find previously, was just beside the Gateway to India and opposite the Taj Hotel. This was the Victory Cafe outside and the Time and Talents Cafe within. It seemed to be mainly for the armed forces, and the kitchen run by Parsees. It was somewhat derelict, right by the water, with rusting iron chairs and tables, and very much like some of the scruffier waterfront cafes in Beirut. It must have had some sort of charitable status, for it was also full of ladies and elderly gentlemen of good family, selling tickets for amateur theatricals and suchlike. It was also next door to the old Bombay Yacht Club, at whose lawns we could peep through gaps in the creeper-covered trellis. Finally, it had the best food of any restaurant we ate in in India.

On each of the several occasions we ate there, we argued why this should be. Each day, the menu changed at lunch, and each evening there was a variety of delicious snacks. Perhaps the good ladies contributed their service, and their cooks, in the kitchen out back, which one could see was only a corrugated iron shed. Each day brought new dishes and fresh revelations; everyone was happy, for the food was neither too hot for some nor too bland for the others, and always enough for our vegetarian. At lunchtime it was crowded with professional people, many of whom we guessed probably worked in the Taj across the way. In the evening the group was more relaxed, with lots of soldiers, but there was the feeling that everyone was there for the same reason – the predictable perfection of its food.

The other exceptional meal we had was at Gaylords. Like Gordons, this was also on ground level, this time with dark red plush with patterns in deep relief, off-white gilded plaster walls, and a very bad quartet banging away far too loud. There were two or three young men in suits with loud ties (the gay lords, perhaps), who were in rank somewhere between the slightly sinister manager and the ordinary waiters. It was Sunday lunch, and I had taken the precaution of asking the day beforehand if they would be open, and would they have lobster. They were, and they did, and we ordered lobster mayonnaise. The lobster was fresh to perfection and even more surprisingly, the mayonnaise too. There was also a gigantic Russian salad with odd pieces of fruit tucked into it. After having eaten the lobster, I could not quite make up my mind what I had had, for its empty carcass did not quite explain its contents. Had I had two halves, or two tails split?

In the afternoon we went to the aquarium, and the answer lay in a deep tank, where a score of Bombay lobsters swum in and out of rocks. They were like a cross between *cigales de mer* and *langoustes* with double spikes almost two feet long probing the water ahead of them. They only had two largish claws, which accounted for the absence of more of them in the restaurant. Seeing them alive I felt a pang of conscience at just having devoured one with such relish; they were very impressive. Also in the aquarium we saw many varieties of local and tropical fish, a small shark, some stingrays again with spikes, this time held straight up behind them like handles, whilst their bodies undulated like carpets blown up at the edges by a fierce wind. There was also an enchanting little fish, with broad bands of grey and dark indigo and a fan-shaped tail. This was called a Koran fish, for on its tail in violet-blue marking on a darker ground was convincingly spelled out in Arabic, 'God is Great'. Its proper name was *Holocanthus semicirculatus*.

After the fish we wandered down on to Chowpatti beach, in full swing on a late Sunday afternoon. On the fine sand, there was every sort of food and entertainment. There were fortune-tellers, folk-doctors, performing monkeys and kite flyers; and a double row of stalls selling *belpuri*, a sweet mixture of cereals and spices, and ordinary rice *puri*, which would be broken open and dipped in tamarind juice. Donkeys raced along the wet strand, and in the distance across the bay rose the new Bombay. To the westwards behind the green banks of Malabar Point and the rich Parsee apartment blocks lay the Towers of Silence, and the vultures, which we never saw.

On the last day after concluding all the formalities concerning our final departure we walked back past one of the most striking of the older buildings in Bombay. This was the headquarters of the Asiatic Society, older than and the predecessor of the Royal Asiatic Society in London. The classical building had once been the Town Hall, designed by Colonel Thomas Cowper between 1821 and 1833. It had Doric columns outside with wooden canopies over the tall windows and just enough ornament on their ends to link them gracefully to the detailing of the stone facade. Inside there was a great hall with a glazed roof supported on Corinthian columns, and lit at either end with domed circular openings in the style of the Pantheon. It was as fine as any Regency building I could think of in England, with the oriental curving wooden canopies providing just the right touch of distinction between East and West.

I had already been back again to the Prince of Wales Museum to look at the Indian miniatures. I had the feeling that when we had been there before I knew too little about India and had been too preoccupied with our prospective travels to do them justice. This time I looked at them more carefully, one by one. This time I also discovered that I was looking at them quite differently, rather as my taste for fiery food had improved over the past two months. I found I could now distinguish not only between the different styles of painting, but also their quality. I found myself fascinated by the construction of the paintings. There was a miniature of a firework display, where the shooting sparks were a dull gold and not in themselves particularly spectacular. But the excitement of the subject was conveyed by simply painting the effect of the firework-light on the ground, which was a chalky white. It was a perfect demonstration of a thesis that is more often true in scholarship than in art. This is that if you want to reveal a central truth, it can be done by a minute examination of evidence which is peripheral but also tangential to it. So after our week in Bombay we really got to like the city very much. After solving the problems of accommodation and food, there was much to entertain all of us on many different levels, and we left feeling there was much more to be done. It therefore came as a shock to us to hear an English teacher of physics who had arrived from Nairobi by plane the same day as ourselves, and had also spent a week waiting for the boat, lecture us on how awful and backward he had found the town. I suppose it is all a matter of perspective, because our own view of Bombay after two months in India, Ceylon and the Maldives was quite different to that when we had first arrived. We kept very quiet.

One of my favourite mementoes of our last week was a sign on a stall below the Customs House, which I had all too many occasions to visit; it read:

HOT MUTTON PATICE

I asked twice on two separate days for some patice; but both times I was told they had not come yet. I was very glad we had.

At last, we set sail on the *Dwarka*, with the wreck of Speedy in the hold. We were ten days at sea, steaming back via Karachi, Muscat, Dubai, Doha and Bahrain, to Kuwait. The voyage was quite uneventful. We arrived early in the morning at the pier in Kuwait, and the wreck was gently lowered on to the sand. There was no sign of El Hoss Company, the agents, but a lone figure came forwards to greet us. This was David Robins, from the American Embassy, who was a friend of Peggy's sister-in-law, who had heard we were coming. He took us under his wing and we stayed in his apartment for the next three days. He was efficient and kind and helped us getting the car through the customs, again with endless visits to offices and formalities. We left Speedy behind in Kuwait, to be shipped directly to Beirut in the next few days. We ourselves booked a Syrian Airlines flight to Damascus.

It was the beginning of Ramadan, strictly observed in Kuwait, at least in public. Office hours dwindled to nothing, and everyone was edgy; this showed particularly in the driving. We made one excursion to the south of the town, and found an abandoned mud-brick site close to the sea, and a single Chinese blue-and-white sherd which might easily have been broken off one of the bowls of which we had an identical piece of from the Maldives.

We flew over the tawny desert to Damascus in the early morning, covering in two hours what had taken us three days in the car. In Kuwait, far below we could see what looked like a lighted matchstick and a black slick snaking away from it; this was oil. Further into the desert there were sand dunes, then a black basalt outcrop, and at last the green blot of the oasis of Damascus. We were in a Caravelle, and we drifted slower and slower across the pock-marked sand until we almost stopped, till touching lightly down.

11

WAR

When we arrived back in Beirut, it was to find the seeds of war were gathering fast. Earlier in the year, before we had left, there had been an incident of no great importance in itself, but which proved to be the catalyst which set alight a bloody civil war, the flames of which took twenty years to quench. A minor politician was leading a rally of fishermen in Sidon one Sunday afternoon, protesting against the sale of the rights to fish the Lebanese coast to a Japanese company. This deal had been negotiated by ex-President Camille Chamoun, leader of the Maronite Christians, and when the politician was assassinated during the rally, it was assumed that he had been responsible for his elimination. Be that as it may, shortly afterwards Chamoun's office in Beirut was dynamited. And shortly after that, a busload of Palestinians from one of the Beirut camps was somewhat illogically wiped out by the Chamounists.

At this juncture, the Palestinians had been in Lebanon for twenty-five years, after their forcible evacuation from their homeland during the creation of the state of Israel in 1948. Living mostly in squalid camps on the southern fringes of Beirut, with other enclaves in the south near Tyre and Sidon, they had been supported by the charity of the United Nations, who provided basic food and education. To the Lebanese they were considered as pariahs, and they heartily wished they would go away. In turn, they had no place in Lebanese society, and quite apart from lacking any rights or hope of citizenship, they were positively victimised; for instance, if you wanted to get a driving licence or any such documentation, it would cost you a great deal more if you were a Palestinian.

The Palestinians were also the scapegoats for anything that upset the delicate balance between the Christian and Muslim communities. Since the independence of Lebanon in 1946, the country was governed by a Christian President and a Muslim Prime Minister, and a coalition of members of parliament representing the infinite variety of religion and ethnic background. In the boom years of the expanding economy in the sixties and seventies there was no place for the underprivileged except in the service sector, and this went for other minority groups such as the Kurds, as well as the Palestinians. The Lebanese averted their eyes to the festering squalor of the various camps which ringed the city and were implanted in the countryside. Indeed, such was the offence caused by one highly visible camp on the main highway to Byblos and other touristic sights in the north, that the municipality built a high wall along the road, with openings every hundred yards or so, so that it was concealed from view. Concealed, but not forgotten, for one of the early highlights of the civil war occurred when the Christian militia (under Dany Chamoun, the ex-President's son) razed the camp to the ground with bulldozers, with the unfortunate inhabitants still in their homes. A week later I shared a taxi with a group of Christians on my way to work in Beirut, and we stopped to have a good look and a laugh.

But in the early days of the war the incidents were sporadic and nobody really believed that they would develop into a full-grown war. Realising that it was only symptomatic of the divided nature of Lebanese society as a whole, further amplified by the colossal gap between the rich and the very poor, with the Palestinians and other minority groups thrown in for good measure, many hands tried to unravel the mess by the simple expedient of backing one particular faction against the rest. Thus the struggle became internationalised, with money and the instruments of war pouring into the country from all directions. With Israel's paramount interest in destabilising the highly successful Lebanese economy, added to the great power interests of the Soviet Union and the United States, let alone the other interested parties in the Arab world and Europe, a major conflagration was inevitable.

Once started, it was almost impossible to reverse, and it can truly be said that it was not until the demise of the Soviet Union that there was any hope in sight. Even today, the peace is an extremely fragile affair.

As far as we were concerned, living in Tabarja, a fishing village fifteen miles north of Beirut in the Christian heartland, we were isolated from the immediate conflict in Beirut. But I had to go to work, and the children had to go to school, both of which meant crossing the then invisible line separating the Christian and predominantly Muslim halves of the city. The American University where I taught, and close to which the children went to school, were both in Ras Beirut. To get there it was necessary to drive along the port, immediately below the heights of Ashrafieh, the Christian stronghold. Apart from occasional checkpoints on either side, to begin with there was no particular problem.

What about Speedy? After we collected the wreck from the airport, we found a garage prepared to restore it, for the not excessive sum of five hundred pounds; but it would, however, take several months to complete. As luck would have it, the garage was exactly on the line dividing the city, just above the Bourg, the central area of downtown Beirut. The weeks passed, and the situation worsened, and we were no longer able to pay occasional visits to see how the work was progressing and inject cash payments for each stage. It then became impossible to get to the garage at all, and the situation along the so-called Green Line became extremely tense. Both sides were firing at each other across the divide, first of all by sniping, and then using rockets and all kinds of explosive devices. The Green Line did, in fact, become green, for as the war progressed weeds and wild flowers and even eventually trees sprung up along the *cordon sanitaire.* On either side the buildings became increasingly bullet-ridden and pockmarked, like some ghastly kind of urban Gruyère. The kidnapping began, and it became dangerous to stray into the territory of the opposing faction; as numerous militias now sprang up, it was not easy to detect who was who. Lacking the car, we were using public transport, either the bus or seats in a *service*, a shared taxi. The Bourg became our interchange; as far as Beirut we used Christian drivers, and from then on to the University, a mile or so, whoever we could find. It was safer to stick together, so we would all leave early in the morning and Peggy would stay in Beirut until it was time to return. Then there were days when the fighting was so bad we could not get into the city at all; and other days, having got there found it impossible to return in the evening, and we were obliged to stay in Beirut. Here we were lucky, for we had the use of a little house in Ras Beirut belonging to friends who were away.

At the end of a year or so, there was a kind of a lull in the fighting and serious talk of a ceasefire. One Saturday I decided we would try to get the car. Peggy and myself got to the Bourg, found one of the mechanics, who tucked a new battery under his arm, and well aware that we were exposed to sniper fire from both sides, made an extremely nervous dash for the garage. Or what was left of it, for only the remains of its walls were still standing; the roof had completely disappeared. But most surprising of all, there was Speedy standing in the ruins, covered with what appeared to be a thick coat of shaving cream. In fact, a bullet had hit the fire-extinguisher on a nearby wall, which had promptly exploded and emptied the entire contents over the car. We scraped it off the windscreen, put in the new battery, and even more surprisingly it started at the first turn of the key. We shot off back to the Bourg at top speed, hardly able to believe our good fortune.

Now we had Speedy back, at least our troubles with public transport were over. The war was not; the cease-fire never materialised and the fighting got more intense. The American University was shelled, a young friend working in the administration, Zahi Khoury, who had been one of my students, disappeared somewhere in the port area driving home to his wife and family in the mountains, never to be seen again. Suha Tuqan, working in the same department and a terrific artist on the side, was shot giving a French journalist a lift home, for not stopping at a checkpoint. My landlord in the village told me proudly that the Christians were stopping all the buses and taxis to Tripoli in the north, and pulling out any Muslims, at the bridge over a deep ravine a mile or so up the road on the autostrada. They were then thrown over the side; more fun, he said, to do it live.

Two incidents particularly stick in my memory. The first involved Henri Pharaon, who I have mentioned early on as one of the initial collectors of Chinese porcelain. I went to call one day to find him alone in his great mansion, in what was fast developing as one of the most dangerous areas in the city. He was not a specially brave man, but he had decided to stay put. As he rightly said, if everyone stayed in their own houses instead of fleeing, many of them abroad to France and Switzerland, things would be settled faster. He had a couple of servants looking after him, one of whom, an Ethiopian Copt, had his throat slit, for no clear reason. On another occasion, two Muslims had escaped from a *service* taxi and had run down the road and asked him for sanctuary, as they were being chased by a Christian gang. He took them in, and rang up Camille Chamoun, who promised to send a tank to rescue them and deliver them to safety. But before this happened the Christian militia broke in and shot them in front of Henri Pharaon's eyes. As he said bitterly, at that moment they were drinking my coffee ... But then he cheered up and asked me if I would like to see his new collection. I could not imagine what he meant, until he led me into the entrance hall, where he had laid out examples of every shell and bullet that had hit his property. With true collector's enthusiasm he had them all catalogued too, and pointed out which were of Israeli, American, Russian, etc. origin. Pharaon did stay put; he tried on innumerable occasions to forge links between the warring factions, and arrange a truce, sometimes successful and sometimes not. He was one of the true heroes of the war.

The other incident involved a friend of both of us, the Emir Maurice Chehab. He was Director of Antiquities and lived with his wife and daughter in the Beirut National Museum, which like our garage was also on the Green Line, a couple of miles further up the road. It was also the semi-official crossing point between the two halves of the city. I rang him one day to ask him if he was all right. Yes, he said, but it's a bit noisy. On the other hand, at least he didn't have to spend much of his time showing VIPs the delights of Tyre and Sidon and other archaeological sites, and he was getting through a load of his own archaeological research for a change. After moving the more valuable objects to a safe place, and encasing the non-portable sarcophagi and suchlike in concrete coffins, he then rang up the leaders on all sides and simply said that he didn't care who won, but the country's antiquities belonged to everyone, and when they were shelling each other would they please mind doing it to the left or right of the museum, but not through the middle. Although he was the scion of a famous feudal Lebanese family, the Chehabs, he was not the slightest bit political, and his imagination and foresight paid off; the national collections did, in fact, survive almost intact.

After the war had been going for a year or so, the authorities decided that the foreign faculty in the American University should leave. Although most of them were shipped out from the airport, which was in the same zone as the University, we were at Tabarja when this decision was taken, and unable to join the main throng. So we piled into Speedy, and drove north through Tripoli and into Syria. Arriving in Aleppo, we left Speedy in the garage of the Baron Hotel under the care of Coco Mazloumian, its famous proprietor. We then took the train for Istanbul, and I remember distinctly waiting at the Turkish frontier for a new engine. It was early December, and across the fertile plains of northern Syria the snow-capped Taurus Mountains glistened in the sunshine. It was so quiet after all the bombs and bangs and horror of Lebanon at war. In Istanbul, we stayed for a day or so, then took the Orient Express for Paris and London, stopping off here or there as the will took us, tracing the path we had followed so many times previously in Speedy and its predecessors.

We were in London for several weeks, until the American University decided it was calm enough for the foreign faculty to return. I went back first of all by myself, then a few weeks later Peggy arrived with Andy; Kathy and Martha we left behind, one at school in the United States and the other in England, at Cranborne Chase. When we had settled in again, one weekend we went to Syria and retrieved Speedy. Back and forth we went again, always travelling the three of us together. Once returning home through Jounieh, a callow Christian youth (he couldn't have been more than twelve years old) stopped us and poked his machine-gun through the window at Peggy, who was driving. She was so outraged that she shouted at him to put the stupid gun down! This could have been the recipe for disaster, but although he didn't understand a word of what she said, he recognised the tone of mother's tongue lashing at him, and sheepishly withdrew his weapon.

Apart from the conflict, the situation became complicated for us in another way. I suppose we were one of the few who were actually moving between both sides on a regular basis, and hearing all the vociferous justifications for each group. We also, after twenty years in Lebanon, had a multitude of friends, Christians, Muslims, Greek Orthodox, Armenians,

Syrians, and certainly Palestinians, and it was not pleasant to hear them all abusing each other. Nor could we take sides but it should be said that we had a strong sympathy for the much-maligned Palestinians. For me, this dated back to my early days in the Middle East, when I was working as a young man at Jericho, as an archaeological draughtsman. This was in 1951, and next to the ancient mound in the Jordan Valley was the largest camp of Palestinian refugees in the Arab world. Some sixty thousand or more, they had fled from the hill villages and towns of Palestine during the 1948 war, imagining they would return a few weeks later when things calmed down. Seventy years later, they still haven't returned.

Those who fled north to Lebanon comprised two distinct groups. There were the relatively affluent Palestinians of the middle class, who quickly found employment in the business sector or as teachers in the university, doctors, lawyers, engineers and so on. At the lower end of the scale were the unskilled villagers, and it was these who were herded into camps, from Tripoli in the north and down the whole coast of Lebanon, in the suburbs of Beirut, Tyre and Sidon.

Although administered by the United Nations, the camps were in fact ghettoes, exceedingly difficult to extract oneself from as the Palestinians were denied any of the automatic rights of normal Lebanese citizens. Not unnaturally they became hotbeds of Palestinian revolutionaries, fuelled by the Palestinian intellectuals who like so many other liberal thinkers in the Arab world found the relatively tolerant attitude of Beirut very accommodating, compared with the repressive regimes of other Arab countries. It was remarkable how little the Lebanese knew about the Palestinian refugees, quite apart from the outside world, during the sixties and later; indeed, I remember the amazement of a Lebanese friend who took it upon herself to penetrate one of the Beirut camps, at the squalor and repression she found just a stone's throw away from one of the more affluent high-rise suburbs. When the war came, the Palestinians were universally demonised for the role they played, culminating in the appalling slaughter of the inhabitants of the Sabra and Chatila camps, carried out by an unholy alliance of the Israeli army and the Lebanese Christians. Just before this, a smaller camp at Tell Zaatar north of Beirut was beseiged. Ironically, these Palestinians had been settled there in the Maronite heartland as a number of them were Christians. The camp lay just off one of the main roads to the mountains, and for several weeks was cut off by Dany Chamoun's militia. With a Palestinian friend, one of Speedy's more honourable trips was to Tell Zaatar, carrying sacks of flour; at this point neither the United Nations nor the Red Cross could get near it, but nobody paid any attention to an open sports car. But thankful as the refugees were, it was to no avail, for just a few days later the camp was overrun by the Christians and every man, woman and child slaughtered.

Life at the University was definitely on a war footing. Apart from its exposed location, many of the students could not cross the Green Line to get to classes, and those who did were preoccupied by the events which were taking place all around. The least that could be said for the Art Department was that teaching drawing, painting and sculpture under such circumstances had a certain therapeutic effect. I was all alone; none of my colleagues had come back, and the Department was run by myself and Isabelle, my loyal Lebanese secretary. One of the most amusing incidents during this period was to find that an American colleague of whom I had always been a little suspicious, had very professionally wired the whole department so that everyone's telephone line could be tapped by him sitting in his office. Whatever his motives may have been, keeping an eye on departmental politics or perhaps eavesdropping on my known Palestinian allegiances, I do not know. We never saw him again, and I heard some months later he was now working in North Korea for the State Department.

The polyglot nature of Beirut meant that it was an obvious centre for espionage, and the American University like many other foreign institutions provided perfect cover. So did journalism, of whom the most notorious exponent was Kim Philby. Sent to Beirut as the *Observer* correspondent after the debacle of the 'Third Man' affair, Kim was everyone's best friend, myself included. He naturally fell in with the liberal, left-wing element amongst the intellectuals, when not hanging out with fellow journalists (and their wives) at the bar of the St Georges Hotel. I remember one party at which he was present, in a smart villa in the foothills of Beirut, given by Miles Copeland. Miles was euphemistically employed as a purveyor of teaching aids, but was in fact running the CIA. The party was on a Friday night, and there was an American, a Russian, a Frenchman, a German and a Lebanese for starters, just like some crazy Irish joke. We watched a pirated copy of Fellini's *8½*, and drank far too much. I realised afterwards it was spy's night out; for just as the artists, writers, doctors, etc. all had their own coterie to relax, so did the spies.

I hasten to add my own presence at this particular party was entirely innocent, and I was in fact the odd man out; I had been invited by Copeland's wife, who was an archaeologist with interests similar to my own.

When Kim finally left for the Soviet Union, quite a few members of the foreign community, British and American, broke cover in their attempts to cope with the scandal, notably in cornering his innocent wife, Eleanor, and making sure she was secure. Some months later, in a sentimental mood, Kim wrote to Walid Khalidy, the leading Palestinian historian and intellectual in Beirut, bemoaning the fact that in their many conversations, they had never really been able to speak their minds. Walid was furious, for he maintained he always had, and declined Kim's invitation to resume their friendship in Moscow, should he ever pass that way.

One speculates on what kind of a role Kim would have played in Beirut if he had not defected before the conflict began. Most journalists covering the war arrived via Damascus and congregated in the Commodore in Ras Beirut, which had replaced the St Georges as a watering hole. Every bang and puff of black smoke provoked fresh analysis of who was doing what to whom. Although movement was circumscribed, the telephone continued to work, and a quick call to the other side of the city could produce results. Although the postal system had virtually broken down, I found that on my way back home to Tabarja I could enter the largely deserted central post office building through the back door, where a single employee was despatching mailbags to the airport. It was simply a matter of finding the one marked 'London' and popping the letter in.

We didn't have a telephone in the house at Tabarja, but there was one in the little grocer's shop just across the road. Sometimes it worked, sometimes not, so our trips to Beirut became increasingly unpredictable, for we were never sure what we would find. Naturally, our families in the United States and England were alarmed by the news of the fighting. We did not hear from Kathy or Martha for several months, until Martha miraculously got through to the village shop from her school at Cranborne Chase, even persuading them to accept a collect call. Finally, we decided that things were so hot that it was better to install ourselves closer to the University, and loading up Speedy, we temporarily abandoned Tabarja for our friends' vacant house in Ras Beirut. It was a tiny old Lebanese house, two storeys high, in a large garden, once with a view of the Mediterranean but now surrounded by high-rise apartments, mostly deserted as their inhabitants had fled. It was relatively safe, as it was over the brow of Ras Beirut and therefore not on the direct line of fire from Ashrafieh and the north. Andy's school, the Collège Protestant, was just next door, and the American University a short walk away. Things got too dangerous for other friends with families living closer to the centre of town, and two of them moved in with us. There was an acute water shortage, and gas and food were in short supply. Our area was also vulnerable after dark to marauding gangs belonging to the different militias, so when night fell we had to cover the windows so no one knew we were there.

Our friends had left an attic full of logs upstairs, so we had plenty of fuel for the open fire, and this turned out to be our kitchen as well when gas was short; I invented what we christened a coat-hanger steak, making use of a large supply of hangers in one of the wardrobes. In the same wardrobe, I found a very pretty model of a missile, painted in attractive colours. I knew our absent host had dealings with a number of Arab countries, and concluded that this was one of *his* teaching aids; I prudently hid it under the wood pile upstairs. This had unfortunate results, for after we had left the house, it was commandeered by a local militia, and they too worked down the wood pile and of course found the missile. A day or so later, our friend arrived in Beirut and turned up at the house, to be confronted with the evidence. He was in the course of attempting to explain it away, with no great success, when luckily there was a diversion; a Jeep rushed up, bearing the recently decapitated body of one of their comrades.

At the beginning of the second summer of the war, the university decided once more it was time to evacuate the foreign faculty. As we were living more or less permanently by now in Beirut, it meant we had to make a quick dash back to Tabarja to clear things up, for we had no idea how long we would be away. After twenty years Tabarja was no longer the friendly little fishing village I had discovered one weekend from Beirut. When I first arrived, as a bachelor, I was alone in the grandest house in the village, built about the turn of the century in classical Lebanese style with a central space flanked by large rooms on either side and a corridor behind running the length of the house, the kitchen and more rooms opening off to the back. The house itself was built right on the beach in the middle of the village, a natural port from which tradition had it that St Paul set sail. The ceiling was twenty-two feet high, and the triple arcade on the front of the house led out onto a narrow balcony with a spectacular view across the

Mediterranean towards the west. On the horizon, there always seemed to be a fishing boat being pulled either to stage left or right on an invisible string. To begin with, I had running water but no electricity, so each evening when it got dark I would light a pressure lamp, and was soon in bed. In fact I began to adopt the rhythm of village life, getting up when it was light and going to bed when it was dark, which made for difficulties many years later when I had to adapt to more normal urban life in London.

There were about two thousand people in Tabarja all told, mostly fishermen or tilling the citrus orchards that swept up the hillside behind; a few commuted to minor jobs in the city. Maronite Christian, there was a little church on the promontory, but such were the goings-on on local feast days that one felt there was a rich pagan heritage not far below the surface. This was the coast of the god Adonis, and up in the hills at the source of streams and rivers the trees were tied with brightly-coloured rags. For a fact, I know we had a weather witch in the village, the mother of two boys who lived in a little fisherman's cottage on the other promontory. She would control the weather for the fisherman, dancing in a trance with her client along a rocky path. It was a night-fishing village, which meant that business started about midnight, and what with the launching of the boats from the pebbly beach, the shouting and swearing and occasional throwing of stones, it was all very lively. I got used to the noise, and again years later living in Central London got alarmed at how quiet it was during the night.

Before I was married, I was adopted by the wife of one of the fishermen across the road who had a little shop. Umm Marie did my washing, cleaned the house (which simply meant hosing down the tiled floor) and kept an eye on things when I was away in Beirut. She was a character in the village, and not someone to cross the path of lightly. Once she heard that visiting royalty were due to pass through the village on their way to the Cedars in the mountains, so she organised all the little girls with plates of rose petals to strew in the path of the visitors. Unfortunately she mistook a passing Mercedes taxi for the royal cavalcade, and more unfortunately still the little girls threw the rose petals and the metal plates at the taxi. The furious driver confronted the outraged Sitt Marie, and during the violent altercation the royals passed by unnoticed.

When I first arrived in the village in the fifties, everyone spoke Arabic and only a handful knew some French. It was a measure of change that when I left twenty years later, half the village spoke French as well as Arabic and also quite a few English as well. More and more people commuted to Beirut, and the Beirutis themselves discovered the weekend delights of Tabarja. This followed the well-known syndrome; first the artist, then the millionaire, then the whole world in general. My millionaire rented the basement below my house and turned it into a sort of garconnière; now on Sundays the view down from my balcony competed as spectacle with that out to sea, with rows of bikini-clad beauties toasting in the midday sun. Little cafes and restaurants sprang up amongst the rocks, and people began to rent rooms in the other houses on the sea. There was still a feeling of total security, and I knew I could go to Beirut for the day and leave the front door open, and no one would enter. But with the coming of the war, this all began to change. Although 100 per cent Maronite, the village was actually sharply divided into two Christian – and opposing – parties. The war, as all civil wars, was an opportunity to settle old scores, and fighting actually broke out in the village itself, even to the extent of blowing up each others' houses. At the same time, the natural harbour served as a port for much larger vessels than fishing boats, shipping in guns and weapons from abroad. I remember one morning waking to my amazement to find a merchant ship moored outside my bedroom window. And attitudes changed as well. The village children, always friendly and polite, turned cheeky, and started screwing the mirror and other vulnerable parts off Speedy, a thing inconceivable in the past. One was now for the first time made to feel an *ajnabi*, a foreigner, perhaps because of my known connection with the American University, perhaps more so because my landlord, Nabil Azzi, was at daggers drawn with the two young men in the fisherman's cottage, and I was in-between.

Anyhow, we got back to Tabarja and packed as best we could. In our absence two tiny bullet-like missiles had struck our bedroom, penetrating twelve inches of solid limestone, smashing the window all over our bed, and ricocheting round the room. Quite small, they lay on the floor in the centre of the room, their points as sharp as when they was fired; one wondered of what they could have been made? The three of us, Peggy, Andy and myself had a last supper and went to bed early, for we knew we had to cross the Green Line early next morning on our way back to Ras Beirut. We loaded up Speedy at dawn, and by the time we got to Ashrafieh it was quite light. I told Peggy and Andy to crouch down as low as possible, and accelerating as hard as I could, made a dash across the hundred or so yards between the Christian and Muslim sectors. Somewhat shaken, we made it safely, but Andy did not emerge from below the back seat. When we got to the house in Ras Beirut, we got him out and into bed; he was in a state, and we moralised about the traumatic effects of war on young children. Later, we found out what had really happened. Apparently he had gone into the kitchen at Tabarja just before we left, and noticing half a bottle of wine left over from the night before, being a tidy child had polished it off. He wasn't traumatised; he was simply drunk.

By this time Speedy was in need of a mechanic and a thorough overhaul, and was coughing and spluttering badly; but she made one last journey to the university, where we stored her three floors down in the underground garage of the university hospital. It was many years before we were to see her again.

12

AFTER THE WAR

It was strange being a refugee in one's own country, and to begin with we were simply waiting for things to calm down so we could return to Beirut and Tabarja. But the weeks became months, and it gradually dawned on us that maybe we were never going to return at all. Nor was this helped by the American University's attitude to their staff, which was simply that if you were not working, we were not going to pay you. Later an ultimatum was issued, and the faculty were offered a lump sum to terminate their contract – which in my case was a tenured, permanent position. For twenty years, I received $22,000. This kept us going for the best part of a year. We were lucky, as we already had a flat in London which meant that at least we had somewhere to live. At the end of the year, I was lucky and offered a post as visiting Professor at the School of Oriental and African Studies. The Chairman of the Department was the formidable Professor Lambton, but she was very kind to me, and encouraged me to get on with my own research in return for a few lectures and supervising recalcitrant doctoral candidates.

Not unnaturally, I began to read around the subject which had first led us to the Indian subcontinent, that is the trade in Chinese porcelain to the West, and the symbiotic relationship between the Near and Far East with a special interest in the maritime routes. I began to pick up the threads of the story in the Near East, and how the imported blue-and-white had not only influenced the indigenous pottery of Syria, Egypt, Persia and Turkey from the fifteenth century onwards, but how Islamic glass and metalwork and the direct intervention of the Muslim community in China had in turn exerted its own influence on the evolution of both the shapes and the decoration of Chinese porcelain. I have already related how this interest in maritime trade led me back to India and Sri Lanka, and almost every year for the next decade I returned, to survey the coastal sites and then to excavate. In this I was very much encouraged by two men who played an important part in planning my research.

The first was Basil Gray, Keeper of Oriental Antiquities at the British Museum. Basil had been a paternal figure since I first encountered him as a young man, when I began to study the Armenian pottery of Kütahya in his department. I discovered that he was as much interested in Chinese art as that of India and the Near East, and Central Asia as well, and that for him 'oriental' meant something that began in the eastern Mediterranean and ended up in the Pacific. This admirably wide-embracing philosophy was that of his department, founded by Basil's predecessor, Laurence Binyon, whose daughter, Nicolette, he married. Basil was particularly intrigued by the Chinese porcelain I had found in Syria, and after the original manuscript was stolen that year in Italy when we lost the Alfa Romeo to an Italian crook, it was he who after a decent interval firmly encouraged me to start cataloguing it all over again. He had also visited us in Lebanon, for he had been invited by the Musée Sursock in Beirut to organise an exhibition of Islamic art, and they both came to stay with us at Tabarja. We took them on a memorable trip to Syria, to Damascus, Hama and Aleppo. Basil was fascinated, and Nicolette had her own passion, which was lettering. She had founded a unique library of calligraphy and lettering at the Central School of Art, and spent a lot of time snapping new specimens in Syria, ancient and modern alike. I remember her dressed modestly in a black *thob*, or hooded robe, ecstatic about an Arabic neon sign in an expresso coffee bar in the scruffy main thoroughfare of Homs.

My second mentor was Gerald Reitlinger, of the same generation as Basil Gray, and an avid collector of both Chinese and Islamic ceramics. I cannot recollect quite how I came to meet him, but he was friendly in a dour sort of way, and lived alone in a Georgian mansion at Beckley in Sussex. He had, like myself, trained as a painter as a young man, and then given it up although he had a considerable talent. He travelled in the Near East, on the most notable occasion with Robert Byron, on the journey which was the genesis of the latter's famous book, *The Road to Oxiana*. Temperamentally they were quite unsuited as companions and they parted company early on, Gerald continuing by himself in the direction of the Caucasus. From his experiences, Gerald wrote a remarkable but less-known work of his own, *A Tower of Skulls*.

He was a widower, and lived by himself at Beckley, ministered to by a housekeeper. For reasons not known, he did not care for the company of women. A number of famous wives were left on his doorstep whilst their husbands were shown his collection. Gerald simply told them, 'I hear there is a good restaurant in Rye', and shut the door firmly in their faces. Gerald was also intrigued by the Chinese porcelain from Syria, and like Basil equally interested in the Islamic angle. He wrote wonderfully well himself, his magnum opus being *The Final Solution*, a history of the Nazi persecution of the Jews. No Zionist, and certainly not a practising Jew, he felt he had a duty to record accurately what had happened leading up to the Holocaust. Having got that out of his system, he then wrote a marvellously entertaining book called *The Economics of Taste*, about rising and falling prices on the art market from the Renaissance onwards. He was an inveterate haunter of the salerooms, and a whole skew of minor dealers whose offerings caught his fancy. Along with Soame Jenyns, he more or less created a fashion for collecting Japanese *kakeimon* during the war years, and his dining room housed it in showcases which he had himself lined with red silk and a stapler. He also liked to mend his own pottery, with disastrous results, as he had a penchant for bleaching it first in Parazone, and then sticking it together with dark brown glue, and in later years the intractable Araldite. Every room in the house was lined from floor to ceiling with shelves of Chinese and Japanese porcelain, Islamic pottery and tiles, Persian miniatures and other *orientalia*. A visit always took a whole day, punctuated by one glass of sherry produced from a locked cabinet, and a rather good traditional lunch with excellent claret, produced by whoever happened to be the reigning housekeeper.

He got through these in quick succession, and there is a famous story of one who would not take the hint and leave. After breakfast, he asked her if she would like to go for a drive with him. The lady foolishly thought this was going to lead to romance, and accepted with alacrity. He drove her twenty miles to West Sussex, into a field, pushed her out and reversed smartly back home. But it was a later housekeeper who was his real undoing. She had lit the fire in the kitchen one evening, the chimney caught and the whole house burned down. The Sussex fire brigade rescued much of his collection, but the final tableau was Gerald sitting on the lawn, in tears, in front of the smouldering ruin. Not surprisingly he died very shortly afterwards. He left his collection to the Ashmolean in Oxford.

When I started on my travels hunting for evidence of the sea routes and trade from the Far East, I tended to report any evidence back to him immediately, rather like a retriever dog. This meant I got some wickedly funny letters back in return, but also full of sound advice, all typed out on a portable, of which he had never bothered to change the ribbon, with multiple corrections and handwritten addenda.

Once at lunch I told him I was going to survey the Coromandel coast south of Madras, and to my surprise he barked out: 'German stoneware!'. I thought he had gone barking mad; until, two months later, on the site of an old Dutch fort at Sadras, there it was, piles of it, and clay pipe stems too. He had, of course, mentally worked out what *ought* to have been there in the early seventeenth century, quite apart from the fact he had quite a collection of German stoneware himself, most of which was in an upstairs bathroom. All the rooms were put to use at Beckley, and once when inspecting a bedroom full of blue-and-white it was clear his daughter and her boyfriend had spent the previous night there; he snorted, particularly when he saw that she had washed out her silk stockings and tied them neatly to dry, one each through the twin handles of an early fifteenth-century moon vase. One final bit of advice I got from Gerald was always to look down holes in towns, where plumbers, gas fitters and suchlike had been at work. His great achievement was in St James' Square, where he had plucked a transitional blue-and-white cup with an Elizabethan silver mount from an electrician's excavation. Later, following in his footsteps, I did just that in Galle, in southern Sri Lanka where there were masses of Chinese sherds and even some Delft six inches below the surface, in a similar trench.

I enjoyed my year at SOAS, but unluckily there was no chance to turn the post into a permanent position, although Ann Lambton did try. Anxious to continue with my research, I wrote to Robert McCormick Adams, an American archaeologist whom I had met and liked in Beirut, who was then Director of the Oriental Institute at the University of Chicago. He replied there were no research positions available, but there was a vacant post for the Curator of the Institute's museum. I applied and suddenly found, a few months later, that we had swapped the Middle East for the Middle West. Chicago was not without its dangers, either. What I had not appreciated was that the city had in fact a black majority, and that there was not a great deal of contact between the black and white communities. The University of Chicago lay some five miles south of the city centre on Lake Michigan, and was literally isolated by a no-man's land of burned out and dilapidated buildings, mostly the result of arson, separating the community from lower-class black slums. Paradoxically, Chicago had the highest and lowest per capita income groups in the entire United States, Kenwood in the north being a wealthy white suburb, and South Chicago the poorest of the poor, only fifteen miles separating them. The square mile or so of the university and its immediate community was one of the few integrated areas in the city, but was prey to crime of all sorts, rape and burglary in particular. We were told there were white telephones on the streets every hundred yards or so, and you only had to pick up the receiver and a police car would come immediately. All in all, it seemed that Beirut had been excellent training for Chicago.

The Oriental Institute was founded in 1919 by James Henry Breasted, an archaeologist and polymath interested in all aspects of the ancient culture and civilisations of the Middle East. It had developed into a world-renowned centre of research, particularly in the languages of the area – ancient Egyptian, Demotic, Assyrian, Akkadian, Hittite and so on – and this was the main thrust of scholarship, with a number of dictionary projects under way. The present building, a gift of John D. Rockefeller to his friend Breasted, was erected in 1931, in an eclectic style quite successfully blending oriental motifs with the thirties idiom. The museum collection on the ground floor was largely the result of Breasted's acquisitiveness during a period when it was possible to purchase antiquities in the Near East with no great difficulty. Although open to the public, it was little known to a wider audience, and as one of the great collections in the world it seemed to me it sorely needed better exposure. The display was somewhat static and inflexible, and the interior of the building dirty and in a general state of disarray. I set about cleaning things up and creating a space where we could have temporary exhibitions, and redesigned the museum shop. This did not go down well with some of the scholars on the second and third floors, who had got used to a dormant museum and didn't much care for the intrusion of the world in general. One of them seriously suggested to me that I put on a display of Roman erotic oil lamps, so that the museum would be x-rated as far as children were concerned. And at the opening reception for my first exhibition, the Director swooped down the staircase from his office on the first floor demanding to know who were all these people.

Nor were my own research interests popular, for although Breasted had embraced the entire history and culture of the Near East, the prevalent feeling during my tenure was that anything after Jesus Christ was modern history. This ruled out my own concern with Islamic art, although the museum did have some remarkable and important holdings of Islamic material, some of which I tentatively edged into the permanent display. As for Chinese porcelain, no one in the university knew anything about it, although the Art Institute downtown had an excellent collection. I did, however, manage to get back to India and Sri Lanka at regular intervals, and from 1980 until 1984 had three seasons' excavations at Mantai. When I moved from the Oriental Institute in 1983, to become Director of the David and Alfred Smart Gallery, the university's fine art museum, things became easier as the field covered ranged from Jesus Christ to contemporary Chicago. And it was at the Smart Gallery that I was able to organise an exhibition which exemplified my special interests. This was *Blue and White: Chinese Porcelain and Its Impact on the Western World*. The theme was to show how Chinese porcelain had influenced both the technique and design of pottery in the west, from the fourteenth century onwards. With material drawn from twenty-seven museums and collections in the United States and Europe, the display emphasised the Chinese originals side-by-side with their Persian, Egyptian, Syrian, Turkish, Italian, French, Dutch, Spanish, Portuguese, German and English copies. There were even some mad Mexican copies of blue-and-white in the seventeenth century, which I found in the basement of the Art Institute of Chicago, and which combined Buddhist and Aztec motifs! Besides a comprehensive catalogue, we also had a two-day symposium; one of the speakers fell by the wayside, and at the last minute was replaced by William Atwell, unknown previously to me. He was basically an economist, and his subject was the impact of Mexican silver on the world markets in the sixteenth and seventeenth century, largely as a result of its shipment to the Far East across the Pacific by the Spanish galleons sailing annually to Manila.

Every date he mentioned for economic reasons had the art historians sitting up, for these were also the dates when particular stylistic changes occurred in both Chinese and Japanese porcelain. The Manila galleons brought back quantities of porcelain on their return to Mexico, much of which was then transhipped from Acapulco overland to Vera Cruz, and then across the Atlantic to Spain. This, of course, explained the genesis of the mad Mexican pottery I stumbled across.

After a decade or so in Chicago, I was invited by Sotheby's in London to become Director of their Islamic Department. Hesitant at first to leave the academic and museum world and become a businessman, I was reassured by Sotheby's that I would be given every opportunity to continue with my own research, publishing and teaching, a promise which was admirably kept. All the same, the bottom line was to make money for Sotheby's, and it was initially a curious feeling when dealing with the general public to be expected to tell them *how much* an object was worth as well as what it was. In the museum world it is forbidden to ever mention value, and to begin with I felt rather like a naughty schoolboy. For business reasons, I began to travel again in the Middle East, to Syria and Jordan, and frequently to Turkey. Beirut was still in the thick of civil war, as indeed was Sri Lanka by now, and was out of bounds. But it so happened that one of my colleagues at Sotheby's, Nabil Saideh, was in close contact with Beirut; Umm Nabil (the mother of Nabil) and his sister Lina were living there. Although born in Manchester, Nabil came from an old Shiite family with property in Lebanon, and he himself had studied at the American University of Beirut before the troubles. At Sotheby's he was Director of the Oriental Manuscript Department, so we saw much of each other.

It was now thirteen years since we had left Beirut, and friends who were still there would from time to time go and have a look at Speedy, hidden away in the underground garage of the university, and report back that the car was dusty but safe. Once I received a letter in Chicago from a Maronite Christian medical student who had spotted it, rather cheekily suggesting that as it would cost me a fortune to have it repaired and pay the back licensing fees, that I should make it over to him. And then one day I received the news that Speedy had disappeared. I was aghast, for although it had never been calm enough to return to Beirut and collect it, I had always imagined that one day I would, and now it was gone. It seemed that a group of young thugs had raided the garage and hijacked Speedy.

About this time, Lina and Nabil's mother came to London on a visit, and I bemoaned Speedy's fate to Lina. She laughed, and said that was the end of that. But the next time we met, she said maybe she might be able to find out exactly what had happened and who had got it when she returned to Beirut. Lina was at that time a well-known personality, as she was the newscaster on Lebanese Television.

She was also extremely brave, for she had to get to the TV building and back again each day to her mother, who was living in the Saideh Building, an apartment block belonging to the family on the southern side of the city. Often she and the engineer would be the only people in the TV station, she reading the news and the engineer taking shelter under her desk and fiddling with the controls. She was one of the leading sources of information about what was going on where during the war, and had many contacts and journalist friends. What she found out was that Speedy had indeed been hijacked, by no less than the Hezbollah. She also promised to try and see if there was any way I might get it back.

It was about this moment that returning all alone one night she was stopped at the end of the road by an attractive young man in a tank who offered to escort her home. This happened on several subsequent nights, and a romance developed between Lina, and Maher. Maher was seriously smitten, and the moment came to break the news to Umm Nabil. This did not go down at all well, as Maher Halabi was a Druse, and as Umm Nabil pointed out firmly, Shiah girls of good family do not marry Druse boys. Lina let her mother simmer for a few days, and then played her trump card, which was to tell Umm Nabil that if she didn't marry Maher, she wouldn't ever marry at all, and would simply stay at home for the rest of her life. Umm Nabil was suitably shocked at the prospect, and graciously gave in.

In the meanwhile Lina felt she really must be sure of Maher's good intentions, and decided to put them to the test. The conversation went something like as follows: 'Maher, do you truly love me?'.

'Ya Lina, of course I do, with all my heart!'. 'Well, if you truly love me, get John's car!'. Maher was not at all daunted by this Herculean task, and set about in earnest. The next I knew in London was a cable from Lina, saying they had located Speedy, and that the Hezbollah were prepared to sell it back to me, for a mere five thousand pounds. I offered half, to include delivery to England, and thanks to Lina and Maher the deal went through. I learned later exactly what happened.

Lina was told to deliver the cash in a brown paper bag, to be left on the back seat of her car, parked on the corniche near the old American Embassy. She was to get out of the car and walk a hundred yards or so to a little cafe on the seaside, and not look back. This she did, and after having a cup of Turkish coffee, returned to the car, to find the money had gone. Collecting Speedy was another matter, as it had been in the Beka'a along with most of the other cars stolen in Beirut. It had been in pretty bad shape when we had left it years ago, and now only had one gear and faulty brakes. Maher and Lina drove it down into Beirut to the best of their ability, the real problem being that they couldn't slow down and stop at the numerous check points and had to shout at the boys to get out of the way.

Some months later I got a call at Sotheby's from Felixstowe, a minor port on the east coast of England. It was the Harbour Master, and he asked me if I was John Carswell, and when I affirmed that I was, he said a container had arrived from Cyprus with something inside belonging to me. I could hardly believe it, for it was Speedy, and the Hezbollah had indeed kept their word. Getting it through H.M. Customs proved to be as tricky, and certainly more expensive, than negotiating with the Hezbollah, but finally we were reunited.

In the meanwhile I had met Charles Morgan, the third generation of the family business. Charles had started off life as a journalist and had worked in the Middle East and in Afghanistan, so he knew something of the political background of the war in Lebanon, and was intrigued to hear Speedy's story. He offered to house it at the factory in Malvern until such time as it could be restored. We went on a sentimental visit, and there it was, looking rather lopsided and forlorn in a shed. The black leather interior was in quite good shape, and lifting up the front seat cushion what should I find underneath but an invitation to the opening of the new Islamic wing at The Metropolitan Museum of Art in New York, and which I must have left in the car when we drove it into the garage for the last time. The Hezbollah had opened it, but as far as I know they didn't attend the reception, although it would have been rather appropriate if they had.

EPILOGUE

What happened later to Speedy? When the car was returned to the Morgan factory, Charles Morgan undertook to restore it when they had time. This took thirteen years. The only communication I had was a phone call: 'Is that you, Mr Carswell? We've got the car in cardboard boxes. Do yer want it left or right?' Tempted to say in the middle, I settled for as was, that is, left-hand drive.

Finally I got a call saying it was finished and would I please come and collect it. I made my final pilgrimage to Malvern to find it was now not white, but cream! The Hezbollah had delivered it dirty and it had been mistakenly interpreted as the original colour. I cast around the workshop for a suitable alternative and settled for British Racing Green.

I now had to get it back to Spain, which meant passing a test for a new driving licence, which I failed. A friend drove it back for me, and Speedy is now asleep in the garage. I now have a car I cannot drive, which joins a Dolmetsch hand-made rosewood descant recorder with ivory fittings I cannot play, and a Whitcomb hand-tailored bicycle I cannot ride. And emphatically no, Speedy is *not for sale*.

Although it was expedient for economic reasons to travel to the Maldives by car, ferry and plane, one should not overlook the academic objective, which was to prove the importance of Male and its singular importance in East–West maritime trade across the Indian Ocean.

The findings were published in detail in 'China and Islam in the Maldive Islands', in the *Transactions of the Oriental Ceramic Society, 1975–1976, 1976–1977*. As I remarked at that time:

> All the sherds from Male, as well as those collected from Ceylon and South India, have been given as a study collection to the Department of Eastern Art in the Ashmolean Museum, Oxford. The sherds have been individually numbered, following the sequence of the catalogue printed at the end of this paper, so that any sherd can easily be retrieved. It is hoped that this combination of printed catalogue, and marked finds deposited in a fixed location, may go some way to solve the perennial problem of publishing sherd material, in a manner that facilitates further study.

INDEX OF NAMES

Adams, Robert McCormick 182
Aractingi, Dr 19
El-Assad, Hafez 14
Atwell, William 185
Azzi, Nabil 177

Bell, H. C. P. 66, 67–8, 104
  and Maldives 70–1, 74, 81, 83–4, 88
Beyhum, Ibrahim 19
Binyon, Laurence 179
Breasted, James Henry 183, 184
Byron, Robert 180

Cardi, Beatrice de 38
Casson, Hugh 157
Caton-Thompson, Gertrude 25
Chamoun, Camille 163, 167
Chamoun, Dany 164, 171

Chehab, Maurice 168
Cheng Hua 94
Cohen, Jackie 130
Copeland, Miles 172
Cosmas Indicopleustes 70
Cowper, Colonel Thomas 160
Curzon, George, Lord 130, 131

da Gama, Vasco 129
Daniels, Tony 9
de Silva, Dr Raja 95, 114
Deraniyagala, Siran 112
Didi, Mohammed 72–3, 75–7, 86, 92, 93

Eskenazi, Giuseppe 18

Fa-Hsien 70
Farouk, Mohammed 57, 115, 116–17
François, M. 2–3

INDEX OF NAMES

Freeman, John 130

Gandhi, Indira 130
Gandhi, Mahatma 123
Gray, Basil 19, 179
Gray, Nicolette 179–80

Halabi, Maher 187, 188
Hourani, George 125

Ibn Battuta 26, 44, 47, 126
  and Maldives 27, 71, 90–1, 94
Ibn Majid, Ahmad 94, 126

Jenyns, Soame 181

Kenyon, Kathleen 111
Khalidy, Walid 172
Khoury, Zahi 167
Kirkbride, Diana 111, 112, 113
Krahl, Regina 20

Lambton, Ann 178, 182
Larsson, Theo 17–18

Ma Huan 94
Manik, Mohamed Hassan 87
Mazloumian, Coco 169
Morgan, Charles 188, 189
Mustafa, Mr 87

Negoomeera brothers 118–19

Pharaon, Henri 15–17, 167–8
Philby, Kim 172
Polo, Marco 26, 91, 106, 126
Pope, John 20
Ptolemy 70

Rahabi, Ezekiel 130, 131
Reitlinger, Gerald 86, 180–2
Robins, David 162
Rockefeller, John D. 183

Saideh, Lina 186–8
Saideh, Nabil 185–6
Sarkis, Elie 13, 14, 15
Sarkis, Khalil 13, 15
Silva, Roland 65, 66, 95, 101
  and Vankalai 107, 111, 114
al-Sirafi, Sulayman 126
Snowdon, Antony Armstrong-Jones, Lord 130
Sulayman 70, 71

Tuqan, Suha 167

Wheeler, Sir Mortimer 24
Willetts, William 106
Woolf, Leonard 62, 110–11

Zahir, Mohammed 82, 85–6, 87, 89
Ziadeh, Farid 23–4